The Leprechauns of Software Engineering

How folklore turns into fact and what to do about it

Laurent Bossavit

The Leprechauns of Software Engineering

How folklore turns into fact and what to do about it

Laurent Bossavit

This book is for sale at http://leanpub.com/leprechauns

This version was published on 2015-06-28

ISBN 978-2-9547455-0-3

Leanpub

This is a Leanpub book. Leanpub empowers authors and publishers with the Lean Publishing process. Lean Publishing is the act of publishing an in-progress ebook using lightweight tools and many iterations to get reader feedback, pivot until you have the right book and build traction once you do.

Tweet This Book!

Please help Laurent Bossavit by spreading the word about this book on Twitter!

The suggested hashtag for this book is #leprechauns.

Find out what other people are saying about the book by clicking on this link to search for this hashtag on Twitter:

https://twitter.com/search?q=#leprechauns

Contents

Preface

This book is a work in progress.

I don't know when, if ever, it will be finished. This is the new normal for books, apparently. It has been the new normal for software for a long time now.

The sample contains two chapters in addition to this preface, and should give you an idea of the topic and my writing style.

I'm still writing further material. If you purchase the book, you are entitled to free updates with all the new material that goes into this book, at no extra charge.

I have no schedule to finish the book, nor a very clear idea of what it will be like when it's done. Probably not too different from what it is now, but assume that any of the book is up for revision.

I'm writing this book because I *must*, not as marketing material or anything else. These are topics that I find myself obsessed with, and I find that the only way I get them out of my system is to write about them. I write about them in various places, and you can probably get your hand on nearly everything I've written for free.

Turning these writings into a book only means that I'm making more of an effort to weave a coherent story out of what learnings I've been able to glean.

By purchasing the book - at any price and in any state - you are supporting me in this effort to understand better what we know about software engineering and why we think we know it.

I appreciate your feedback in any form: cold hard cash, a pat on the back, a piece of gentle or harsh criticism. You're even welcome to tell me what an idiot I am (and I may ignore you).

Thank you.

Chapter 1: Software Engineering's telephone game

The software profession has a problem, widely recognized but which nobody seems willing to do much about. You can think of this problem as a variant of the well known "telephone game", where some trivial rumor is repeated from one person to the next until it has become distorted beyond recognition and blown up out of all proportion.

Unfortunately, the objects of this telephone game are generally considered cornerstone truths of the discipline, to the point that their acceptance now hinders further progress.

It is not that these claims are outlandish in themselves; they started as somewhat reasonable hypotheses. The problem is that they have become entrenched as "fact" supposedly supported by "research", and attained this elevated status in spite of being merely anecdotal.

How we got there

One of the ways that anecdote persists is by dressing itself up in the garments of proper scholarship. Suppose you come across the following claim for the first time:

> Early results were often criticized, but decades of
> research have now accumulated in support of the
> incontrovertible fact that bugs are caused by bug-
> producing leprechauns who live in Northern Ire-
> land fairy rings. (Broom 1968, Falk 1972, Palton-
> Spall 1981, Falk & Grimberg 1988, Demetrios 1995,
> Haviland 2001)

Let's assume that this explanation immediately appeals to you:
it makes sense of so many of the things you've seen in software
engineering! The proliferation of bugs in the face of huge efforts
to eradicate them; their capricious-seeming nature - why, that is
very leprechaun-like!

Of course, you, my reader, may be the kind of hard-headed
skeptic who absolutely and definitely dismisses the idea that
fairies and leprechauns exist at all. If so, please allow that
there exists the kind of person who would be persuaded by a
leprechaun-based explanation; but who, while an open-minded
person, nevertheless thinks that it is important that explanations
be adequately backed by evidence.

Surely you agree that this claim would be convincing to someone
like that, since it cites so many respected authors, and papers
published in peer-reviewed journals.

As it happens, there are many ways this citation style can be
misleading, even without outright fabrication or evil intent:

- the papers are not really empirical research
- the papers support weaker versions of the claim
- the papers don't support the claim directly, but only cite
  research that does

- the more recent papers are not original research, but only cite older ones
- the papers are in fact books or book-length, and you'll be looking for a needle in a haystack
- the papers are obscure, hard to find, out of print or paywalled, and thus hard to verify
- the papers are selected only on one "side" of an ongoing controversy

Surface plausibility

When we look closely at some of the "ground truths" of software engineering - the "software crisis", the 10x variability in performance, the cone of uncertainty, even the famous "cost of change curve" - in many cases we find each of these issues pop up, often in combination (so that for instance newer opinion pieces citing very old papers are passed off as "recent research").

Because the claims have some surface plausibility, and because many people use them to support something they sincerely believe in - for instance the Agile styles of planning or estimation - one often voices criticism of the claims at the risk of being unpopular. People like their leprechauns.

In fact, you're likely to encounter complete blindness to your skepticism. "Come on," people will say, "are you really trying to say that leprechauns live in, what, Africa? Antarctica?" The leprechaun-belief is so well entrenched that your opposition is taken as support for some other silly claim - your interlocutors aren't even able to recognize that you question the very terms upon which the research is grounded.

For instance, when I argued against the "well-known fact" of 10x variations in software developers' productivity, the objection I often met was "do you really believe that all developers have the same productivity?" Very few people can even imagine not believing in "productivity" as a valid construct.

Leprechaun spotting

Leprechauns come in many forms, which I'll call tacit, folklore and formal. We need to deal with these various forms differently.

Tacit

Some Leprechaun claims have become so pervasive in software engineering discourse that they don't even appear *as* claims any more.

For instance, people who are trying to hire "rockstar" or "ninja" programmers are probably influenced by a tacit belief in the supposedly large variations in programmer productivity, even if they don't explicitly say that they are looking for a "10x productivity programmer". There is a hidden inference at work: "there exist programmers who are ten times as productive as the average, *therefore* it is a profitable investment for me to go to great expense to find one of these".

Another example might be someone who defends Agile testing techniques, such as Test-Driven Development (TDD), because "they reveal defects early". There is a hidden inference too, which relies on the "well-known fact" that software defects are more costly to fix the later they are detected - and *therefore* TDD lowers costs by catching defects early. Unfortunately, this claim on the cost of fixing defects is at best problematic, as we'll see later on.

Folklore

In many cases, the claims are only secondary. They are reproduced in an article, a blog post or a Powerpoint presentation, often by someone who hasn't read - in fact hasn't even looked at - any of the original references.

Here the inference is explicit: there is a point being made, and the claim is offered in support of the point. It can even be the same point as when the claim is tacit, such as the importance of hiring rockstar programmers or the great value of TDD.

Quite frequently, the Leprechaun claim is only ancillary to the main argument: the author has other reasons for believing in the conclusion they are presenting, and the claim is mostly there as a bit of window-dressing.

Formal

Lastly, there is the case of the primary author: someone who did the bibliographical footwork in the first place, should have known better, and is causing a leprechaun-belief to spread.

Whether we like it or not, software practitioners pay scant attention to academic writing about software development. Rather, most of the insights we take for granted come from authors who have a knack as *popularizers*. They play more or less the same role as popular science journalists with respect to the general public.

Science journalism is a fine and important thing, but it has a well-known failure mode: sensationalism, where the lure of an attention-grabbing headline causes writers to toss caution to the wind and radically misrepresent a claim.

The examples I've examined (the cone of uncertainty, the 10x variability, the cost of change curve, etc.) strongly suggest that we should raise our expectations of rigor in software engineering writing, especially writing that popularizes research results.

What you can do

This book is intended as a handbook of skeptical thinking and reading, with worked-out examples.

What I want you to take away from reading the book is a set of reflexes that you will call on whenever you come across a strong opinion about software development, whatever "camp" or "community" or "school" that opinion comes from.

It will probably be easiest to apply these reflexes against what I've called the "folklore" and "formal" version of Leprechaun claims: when you come across them in an article, blog or book, and the claim is spelled out explicitly.

It isn't necessarily the best of ideas to always call out such claims, especially if you are overly antagonistic about it; you may end up being seen as a "troll" - someone more interested in winning arguments than in the truth of things. However, these false claims *will* keep spreading unless somehow kept in check. I cannot any longer accept that it's better to keep quiet and not rock the boat.

The best approach is probably to keep track of where the *best* and *most even-handed* treatments of these various claims reside, and to respectfully point people to them. I hope that this book serves as one such source - but I'm under no illusion that I can deal with even a substantial fraction of all bogus claims within the space of a single book.

The hardest step

The real challenge will be to apply these reflexes *to your own beliefs*.

An inspiring example

Graham Lee is the author of "Test-Driven iOS Development" (Addison-Wesley, 2012). Page 4 of his book includes a table which reproduces a claim about the "cost of defects", which we'll be examining in detail in a later chapter.

In september 2012, after reading an early draft of *Leprechauns*, Graham published a retraction in the following terms: "I made a mistake. [...] I perpetuated what seems (now, since I analyse it) to be a big myth in software engineering. I uncritically quoted some work without checking its authority, and now find it lacking."

Graham not only took seriously my warning about the "cost of defects" claim. He actually went looking for the actual evidence and made his call on that basis, rather than taking my word for it. That's the kind of behaviour I'd like to see more of.

I hold out little hope that people can, in general, convince *others* to let go of specific pet notions. Speaking out against belief X may not do much for those who currently hold belief X strongly enough that they are writing or blogging about it, although there will hopefully be some happy exceptions like Graham.

However, I do believe that if we manage to raise our overall level of "epistemic hygiene", we can prevent Leprechauns from spreading in the first place. Like its real-world counterpart, epistemic hygiene can be vastly improved by the use of specific techniques that aren't hard to learn, like washing hands.

That's what's coming next. Onwards!

Chapter 2: The Cone of Uncertainty

You may have come across something called the "cone of uncertainty".

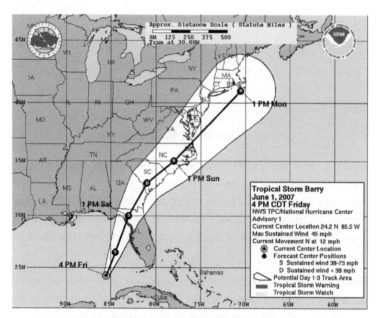

Cone of uncertainty, meteorological version

There are several graphics out there called that. The one with the widest recognition is probably the one used to model the future paths of hurricanes.

A more obscure one is the "binomial tree" used in the theory of financial options.

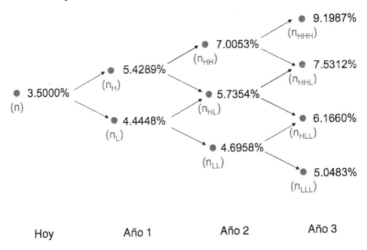

Cone of uncertainty, financial version

In both cases this is diagrammed from a present-time perspective, with the cone widening toward the future. We have some certainty about what is going to happen a few seconds from now - in all likelihood it will be whatever is happening now, more or less. And the further into the future we try to peek, the murkier it becomes.

What we're going to discuss - and what has come to be accepted as one of the "well known truths" of software engineering, more specifically of software project management, is the following "inverted" cone, popularized by Steve McConnell after a diagram originally from Barry Boehm.

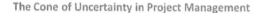

The Cone of Uncertainty in Project Management

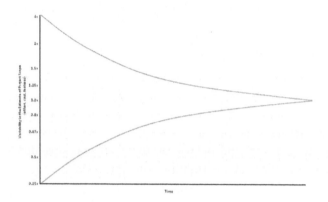

Cone of uncertainty, project management version

This is diagrammed from a future-time perspective, and shows uncertainty as a symmetrically widening range as we move further toward the present, which (given the usual convention for diagrams with a time axis) is on the left of the figure.

How to feel foolish in front of a class

The diagram became well-known when it was published in Steve McConnell's "Rapid Software Development", in 1996. McConnell cites a 1995 Boehm article as the source, but the diagram can in fact be found as early as 1981 in Boehm's famous book "Software Engineering Economics".

McConnell's book is where I first came across the Cone, and it struck me as entirely plausible. I started using it to illustrate the perils of project planning. I distinctly remember one particular occasion when I was instructing a group of software engineers on the topic of "agile planning", and I started drawing a picture of the cone of uncertainty.

And I stopped dead in my tracks.

Because I'd just realized I hadn't the foggiest idea what I was talking about, or how I'd know if it made sense. I was just parroting something I'd read somewhere, and for once trying to explain it wasn't helping me understand it better, it was just making me confused. And all I wanted to say anyway was "don't trust estimates made at the beginning of a project".

Making sense of the picture

What is odd, to any experienced software engineer, is that the Cone diagram is *symmetrical*, meaning that it is equally possible for an early estimate to be an over-estimate or an under-estimate. This does not really square with widespread experience of software projects, which are much more often late than they are early.

If you think a little about it, it can get quite puzzling what the diagram is supposed to *mean*, what each of its data points represents. A narrative interpretation goes like this: "very early in the project, if you try to estimate how long it will take, you're likely to end up anywhere within a factor of 4 of what the project will eventually end up costing". So a 1-year project can be estimated as a 3-month project early on, or as a 4-year project.

Even after writing a first cut of requirements, a 1-year project can be estimated as a 6-month project or as a 2-year project.

It's not clear that this latter case it at all common: a project that has reached this phase will in general take *at least* as long as has been planned for it, an instance of Parkinson's Law. The Cone suggests that the distribution of project completion times follows a well-behaved Gaussian. What the Cone also suggests is that the "traditional" project management activities help: "By the time you get a detailed requirements document the range of uncertainty narrows considerably." And the Cone suggests that uncertainty inevitably narrows as a project nears its projected release date.

Widespread experience contradicts this. Many projects and tasks remain in the "90% done" state for a very long time. So if you wanted a diagram that truly represented how awful overall project estimation can be, you would need something that rep-resented the idea of a project that was supposed to be delivered next year, for 15 years in a row. (Yes, I'm talking about Duke Nukem Forever.)

Getting to the facts

Boehm's book is strongly associated with "waterfall" style project management, so for a long while I resisted getting the book; I'd verified earlier by looking at a borrowed copy that the diagram was indeed there, but I wasn't really interested in digging further.

What I seemed to remember from that brief skim was that the diagram arose from research Boehm had done at TRW while

building his large quantitative database which forms the basis
for the COCOMO cost-modeling framework, and which is the
book's main topic.

I assumed that the diagram was the "envelope" of a cluster of data
points obtained by comparing project estimates made at various
times with actuals: some of these points would fall within the
Cone, but the ones farthest from the original axis would draw
the shape of the Cone if you "connected" the dots.

After seeing the Cone turn up in blog post after blog post, for a
number of years, I finally broke down and ordered my own copy.
When it arrived I eagerly turned to p.311, where the diagram is
discussed.

And found a footnote that I missed the first time around:

> These ranges have been determined **subjectively**,
> and are intended to represent 80% confidence limits,
> that is 'within a factor of four on either side, 80% of
> the time'.

Emphasis mine: the word "subjectively" jumped out at me. This
puzzled me, as I'd always thought that the Cone was drawn from
empirical data. But no. It's strictly Boehm's gut feel - at least
that's what it's presented as in the 1981 book.

The telephone game in action

And then I chanced across this bit from a bibliography on
estimation from the website of Construx (Steve McConnell's
company):

Laranjeira, Luiz. 'Software Size Estimation of Object-Oriented Systems,' IEEE Transactions on Software Engineering, May 1990. This paper provided a theoretical research foundation for the empirical observation of the Cone of Uncertainty.

Wait a minute. *What* empirical observation?

Curious, I downloaded and read the 1990 paper. Its first three words are "the software crisis". (For a software engineering leprechaun-doubter, that's a very inauspicious start; the "crisis" being itself a software engineering myth of epic proportion - possibly *the* founding myth of software engineering. We'll come back to that in a later chapter.)

The fun part is this bit, on page 5 of the paper:

Boehm studied the uncertainty in software project cost estimates as a function of the life cycle phase of a product. The graphic in Fig. 2 shows the result of this study, which was empirically validated (3, Section 21.1)

The reference in parentheses is to the 1981 book - in fact precisely to the section I'd just read moments before. Laranjeira, too, takes Boehm's "subjective" results to be empirical! (And "validated", even.)

Laranjeira then proceeds to do something that I found quite amazing: he interprets Boehm's curve mathematically - as a symmetrical exponential decay curve - and, given this interpretation plus some highly dubious assumptions about object-oriented programming, works out a table of how much up-front

OO design one needs to do before narrowing down the "cone" to a desired level of certainty about the schedule. Of course this is all castles in the air: no evidence as foundation.

Even funnier is this bit from McConnell's 1996 book "Rapid Software Development":

> Research by Luiz Laranjeira suggests that the accuracy of the software estimate depends on the level of refinement of the software's definition (Laranjeira 1990)

This doesn't come right out and call Laranjeira's paper "empirical", but it is strongly implied if you don't know the details. But that paper "suggests" nothing of the kind; it quite straightforwardly *assumes* it, and then goes on to attempt to derive something novel and interesting from it. (At least a couple later papers that I've come across tear Laranjeira's apart for "gross" mathematical errors, so it's not even clear that the attempt is at all successful.)

So, to recap: Boehm in 1981 is merely stating an opinion - but he draws a graph to illustrate it. At least three people - McConnell, Laranjeira and myself - fall into the trap of taking Boehm's graph as empirically derived. And someone who came across McConnell's later description of Laranjeira's "research" should be forgiven for assuming it refers to empirical research, i.e. with actual data backing it.

But it's leprechauns all the way down.

Controversy

In 2006 my friend and former colleague on the Agile Alliance board, Todd Little, published empirical data in IEEE Software that contradicted the Cone of Uncertainty. (Such data can be hard to come by, if only because it's hard to know what "officially" counts as an estimate for the purposes of measuring accuracy Todd used the project manager's estimates, included in project status reports).

Todd's article immediately generated a controversy, which is precisely what we should expect if the Cone of Uncertainty belongs to the "folklore" category - it is a belief that is hard to let go of precisely because it has little empirical or conceptual backing. It has *perceptual* appeal, insofar as it supports a message that "estimation is hard", but it also has very, very misleading aspects.

Apparently as a result of the controversy, and in a further departure from the original concept from Boehm, McConnell insisted strongly that the Cone "represented a best case" and that in fact, in addition to the Cone one should envision a Cloud of Uncertainty, shrouding estimates until the very end of the project. Metaphorically one "pushes" on the Cloud to get at something closer to the Cone.

By then though, that model has lost all connection with empirical data: it has become purely suggestive. It has no predictive power and is basically useless, except for the one very narrow purpose: providing an air of authority to "win" arguments against naive software managers. (The kind who insist on their teams committing to an estimate up front and being held accountable for the estimate even though too little is known.) But we should not be interested, at all, in winning arguments. We should be interested in what's true and in what works.

The "Cone" isn't really a good pictorial representation of the underlying concept that we want to get at (which is really a probability distribution). It has drifted loose from what little empirical moorings it had thirty years ago.

What to make of all this?

First, that there is a "telephone game" flavor to this whole thing that is reminiscent of patterns we'll see again, such as the claimed 10x variation between software developers' productivity. One technical term for it is "information cascade", where people take as true information that they should be suspicious of, not because they have any good reason to believe it but because they have seen others appear to believe it. This is, for obvious reasons, not conducive to good science.

 Second, the distinction between empirical and conceptual science may not be clear enough in software engineering. Mostly that domain has consisted of the latter: conceptual work. There is a recent trend toward demanding a lot more empirical science, but I suspect this is something of a knee-jerk reaction to the vices of old, and may end up doing more harm than good: the problem is that software engineering seems bent on appropriating methods from medicine to cloak itself in an aura of legitimacy, rather than working out for itself methods that will reliably find insight.

Third, I wish my colleagues would stop quoting the "Cone of Uncertainty" as if it were something meaningful. It's not. It's just a picture which says no more than "the future is uncertain", which we already know; but saying it with a picture conveys misleading connotations of authority and precision.

If you have things to say about software estimation, think them through for yourself, then say them in your own words. Don't rely on borrowed authority.

 Key points

Before quoting an "authority" or "well-known fact" in our field, be sure to apply basic critical thinking. One formulation I like is by James Bach: "Huh? Really? So?[1]"

That is, *Huh?*, do I really understand the claim? Can I rephrase it in my own words? *Really*, is it in fact true? Can I locate the evidence behind the claim? And finally, *So?* or *So what?*, does anything important depend on the claim being true or not?

Finally, remember that if "a picture is worth a thousand words", a meaningless picture wastes the equivalent of two pages or ten minutes of speech!

---

[1] http://how-do-i-test.blogspot.fr/2011/08/huh-really-so.html

Chapter 3: Why you should care about empirical results

Wherever I go, people tend to tell me that they feel that "academic" research into software engineering is largely irrelevant to their work. Greg Wilson, editor of the 2010 book *Making Software* which rounded up some of the best empirical research in the field, later asked[2]:

> When is the last time you read something in an ACM or IEEE journal that changed how you program or the tools you use? Ever?

"Never", answered Jorge Aranda, who added: "[for researchers], this should be something to be ashamed of." Wilson and Aranda went on to start a very interesting blog[3], "*It will never work in theory*", dedicated to bridging this gap between practice and theory. This is a wonderful effort, and I can't recommend it enough. My concern is that the only people likely to read (and more importantly, comment on) that blog are people already convinced.

---

[2]http://catenary.wordpress.com/page/2/
[3]http://neverworkintheory.org/about.html

We still need to gnaw this bone a little more to get at its marrow: why should we *care* at all about research, especially experimental results?

The perils of empirical research

My colleague "Uncle" Bob Martin, when he gives talks or lectures on topics such as "clean code" or "Test-Driven Development", makes much[4] of the story of Semmelweis. In short, Ignaz Semmelweis was a physician, who, in the 19th century when germ theory was still unknown, noticed the higher rates of women dying in childbirth in certain wards, and made the then-unintuitive connection with the fact that doctors in the same hospitals would often go straight from the dissecting room, where they had been dissecting corpses in the name of science, to "assisting" these women in delivery.

What's arresting and important about this story is that Semmelweis, despite having shown conclusive experimental evidence for the effectiveness of hand-washing in reducing mothers' deaths, faced extreme resistance to his ideas from the scientific establishment of the time, to the point where he basically went into depression from which he never recovered, dying in a mental institution before reaching his fifties. It took two more decades (and many avoidable deaths) before the practice of hand-washing before patient contact became mandatory for physicians.

This is a disturbing and fascinating story, and I understand why Bob likes to tell it. Bob argues that software professionals today failing to at least *learn* and *try* test-driven development

---

[4]http://www.computer.org/csdl/mags/so/2007/03/s3032-abs.html

are showing the same kind of disregard for the very real and very painful problems of software development (low quality, buggy software) that Semmelweis' contemporaries showed to the suffering and deaths of mothers - only because there wasn't yet a fully worked out theory of infectious disease via germs.

There are, however, several problems with this parallel, not the least of which that the data on test-driven doesn't quite measure up to that on hand-washing: "a survey of all of the studies that have been done on TDD have shown that the better the study done, the weaker the signal as to its benefit" (Greg Wilson, commenting on the TDD chapter in "Making Software".) And quite clearly we know a lot more today about scientific research, and in particular about experimental design and statistical validation, than we did in the 19th century.

Can so many researchers be wrong? Is TDD, then, only a mirage? Well... It's not quite that simple.

Discipline envy

A lot of research in software engineering strikes me as hopelessly naive in one of two ways. Most of it fails entirely to account for the social and belief aspects altogether. It looks at its object of inquiry as if it was entirely material and inert; as if "software" was some kind of naturally occurring substance, the properties of which can be revealed in the equivalent of a test tube.

The more interesting but in some ways more distressing part of software engineering research borrows its experimental design approach from medicine and calls itself "evidence-based". Too often though this seems to be a matter of "discipline envy" and scientific status games, of who can use the most impressive-sounding statistical method to analyze data that turns out - on closer inspection - to be useless as empirical evidence, because of some gross conceptual or methodological flaw.

Take a recent study[5], *Comparing the Defect Reduction Benefits of Code Inspection and Test-Driven Development.*

There is one thing that needs to be said first, before we get on to the science, and even if this seems like a relatively trivial complaint: it's really a shame that most readers will have to pay $19 to get the PDF with the full text of the study, because the abstract *really* isn't the whole story. (There's more to say about the economics of academic publishing, some of which was eloquently summarized in George Monbiot's article *The Lairds of Learning*[6]; these issues eventually sparked a boycott of well-known publisher Elsevier.)

The paper "is a quasi-experiment comparing the software defect rates and implementation costs of two methods of software defect reduction: code inspection and test-driven development". The main claim is that the Inspection group turned in code that had fewer defects than the TDD group, and the authors claim, at the p=0.05 level of statistical significance which is the accepted norm (in medical research, for instance), that this is a reliable result.

But wait! That's only the abstract. If you go to the trouble of reading the whole paper, you learn that this is only true, statistically speaking, for "adjusted" defect counts. When the authors look at "unadjusted" defect counts there is no statistically

---

[5]http://doi.ieeecomputersociety.org/10.1109/TSE.2011.46
[6]http://www.monbiot.com/2011/08/29/the-lairds-of-learning/

significant difference: "based on the unadjusted defect counts, we would reject hypotheses H1 and H2". (This is a common problem in such studies, pointed out[7] decades ago: noise swamps out signal - we will come around to this when we examine the evidence, or lack thereof, for "10x programmers".)

What does "adjusted" mean? It means basically that the Inspection students get credited not only for the bugs they fix during the one-week period after developing their code; they also get credited for all the bugs *they didn't fix*, that were found during inspection. This effectively stacks the deck in favor of Inspection over TDD, and it's easy to suppose that this entirely accounts for the supposedly statistically significant difference between the two groups.

(The authors justify this procedure on the grounds that a well-run Inspection process would keep inspecting and fixing until all bugs found in the first Inspection round were in fact fixed. But that doesn't change the fact that the Inspection group effectively gets to do a lot more testing than the TDD group; it's not so surprising that this results in fewer defects.)

So what's going on here, really?

Science and reality

The Inspection vs TDD study is burdened with further flaws: the participants in the TDD group were given barely more than one hour of TDD training, for instance, on top of the usual problems with studies which look at "convenience samples" -

---

[7]http://dx.doi.org/10.1109/PROC.1981.12088

that is, graduate students enrolled in the researchers' course. But really, the problem here is that the whole study is just too vulnerable to all kinds of biases, both the researchers' and the participants'.

Consider Philip K. Dick's idea, "Reality is that which, when you stop believing in it, doesn't go away." How does that strike you? Obviously true? Uncontroversial? To me this captures one essential aspect of experimental science - reality responds in certain ways when you prod it, whether you believe in what you're seeing or not. "Fact" is the name we give to this stubbornness of reality, its refusal to be persuaded by what we prefer to believe. So it goes for matter and gravity, right up to the strange and counterintuitive properties of light and tiny particles.

But then comes the niggling thought that some aspects of reality "go away when you stop believing in them", or more broadly are significantly affected by how much and in what ways we believe in them, countering naive reductionism. Some of the examples that come to mind are romantic love, social status, money, fashion or art. You can still get at facts about these things, but by a much more tortuous route than you get facts about the laws of physics.

Remember the TDD/Semmelweis connection? The bigger issue there is that while germs are very much in the "don't go away if you stop believing in them" category, that's much less true of these things we call[8] "bugs". (The "better" studies of TDD mentioned above show some of the naivete I believe is one of software engineering's deeper problems; the "anecdotal" reports on which TDD enthusiasts base their recommendations may not

---

[8]http://www.ayeconference.com/entomology/

pass muster as "proper" research but may well get at more useful insights than the academic research.)

The thing is, more aspects of reality than we'd like to believe belong in the latter category. The so-called "placebo effect" is a well-known illustration, and there are many subtleties to designing experiments that take these effects into account. For instance in medical research[9] on psychoactive drugs: "many antidepressant trials have serious methodological weaknesses, including the unblinding of raters due to the common side effects of these drugs compared with the inert sugar pill".

Where to go from here

In fact, researcher John Ioannidis garnered much attention a few years back with an admittedly provocative headline[10]: *Why Most Published Research Findings Are False*. Far from being a shining example to look up to, medical research turns out to have its own deep-seated problems!

I am not making this point to dissuade anyone from taking an interest in software engineering research - far from it. Whether you think of yourself as a software engineer, a craftsman, or a "code monkey", I think you are making a twofold mistake if you dismiss the work of academic researchers as irrelevant.

First, you are failing to develop yourself as a professional; you are missing out on some insights that would be useful to you, but more importantly you are failing to engage with some important

---

[9]http://www.srmhp.org/0201/media-watch.html
[10]http://www.plosmedicine.org/article/info:doi/10.1371/journal.pmed.0020124

issues; you are delaying progress not just for yourself but for your professional community as a whole.

Second, you are taking the risk of being blindsided. Right or wrong, changing scientific consensus will eventually have *some* impact, small or large, on the way you work. To turn a blind eye to where this consensus is going is to forfeit some of your right to take part in the conversation about how you work.

As practitioners, it is both in our interest and within our responsibility to pay attention to research. This includes not just the findings of such research, but also its processes and its institutions. Read research papers; find out what's happening in that world and why it's not more relevant to your work; weigh in; make your voice heard.

It is becoming increasingly clear that we must improve the quality of the conversation between researchers and practitioners. To make research more relevant, we must find new models and new methods, more appropriate to locating and then confirming hypotheses about software development, and we must make this a joint effort, with both practitioners and academics involved. And to do all that, we may need to abandon outdated paradigms - perhaps even move on from the "software engineering" label.

Key points

Research matters. We're less likely to shoot our-
selves in the foot when we base our decisions on
solid evidence, and much more when we follow
whim, fashion or whoever spoke last or the loud-
est.

However, one crucially important and usually
overlooked fact of software development is that
it involves *people*, and academic research on the
topic has by and large failed to acknowledge this.

Therefore, while it's indispensable for practitioners to keep abreast of research results in the field,
and for academics to engage with practitioners,
we need always to maintain a critical attitude
towards what we read.

Chapter 4: The messy workings of scientific discourse

The trouble with opinions is that everyone has their own; you can always find one to suit any given prejudice. "Test-driven development reduces defect count", says one expert; "test-driven development will wreck your architecture", says the next.

Knowledge cannot be disseminated merely by everyone having a blog of their own. Blogs are great for voicing opinions - are they ever - and for having debates, but it's unhealthy for debates to go on forever. We look to scientists for settling them.

One debate (if it can be called that) which has gone on for too long without a satisfactory resolution concerns programmer productivity and the often quoted "observation" or "fact" that the best programmers are 10 times better than the worst. We will start examining this observation closely in the next chapter.

This chapter is about why some "facts" refuse to die, and about how to avoid being fooled by opinion disguised as scientific "fact". We start, therefore, with some observations on science and facts.

Modalities

Bruno Latour is one of the keenest observers I know of the work that scientists really do, and one of the most punctilious in clearing away the myths and misconceptions about how science is in fact done. I have found good use in some of the tools he created to assess the status of an *ongoing* debate about a matter that falls within the purview of science, one that hasn't been settled - what he calls a controversy[11].

(I stumbled across Latour when someone recommended Aramis[12], a book which thoroughly changed the way I saw and thought about software projects, even though its subject is public transportation. I have been recommending it ever since to colleagues and friends involved in software in any capacity; it ranks near the top of my list of must-read books for the profession. It's remarkable not just for Latour's determined and meticulous manner of observation and of getting to the bottom of things, it also reads like a detective story.)

Latour draws attention in particular to the role of **modality**[13] in scientific discourse. The concept has complicated ramifications but is really simple at its core, as we'll see by walking through an example. Start with a statement of fact, such as "water boils at 100 degrees celsius". A modality is a way to alter the meaning of this statement, not by modifying but by extending it: "if I remember right, water boils at 100 degrees celsius" expresses uncertainty, whereas "everyone knows that water boils at 100 degrees celsius" implies authority. "Scientists know that water

---

[11]http://www.mappingcontroversies.net/
[12]http://en.wikipedia.org/wiki/Aramis,_or_the_Love_of_Technology
[13]http://en.wikipedia.org/wiki/Linguistic_modality

boils at 100 degrees celsius" lends a somewhat different authority to the same statement, implying that knowledge of it may be restricted to a select few.

Citation as modality

In the practice of science, a **publication** takes on the role of an extended modality. A researcher may wish to state a conclusion: "water boils at 100 degrees celsius". Convention dictates that he should initially add various hedges to his conclusion: "subject to the threats to validity mentioned above, given our results it seems legitimate to claim that the boiling point of H2O under the experimental conditions lies, for a 95% confidence interval, within 0.01 of a 100 degrees celsius". The rest of the publication (or "paper") amplifies these precautions.

A lone experiment or study rarely being sufficient to establish a scientific fact, further "papers" are expected to build on an initial work, whether by the original author or by other researchers. One prerequisite is that the initial work be *interesting*; that often serves as a first filter, and probably a fair fraction of all scientific work is never cited by other researchers. Thus, **citations** play a crucial role in the acquisition by some statement of the status of a "scientific fact".

Now you can think of a citation as being itself a modality, one that can express a degree of confidence: "Preliminary work by Jones (2001) suggests that the boiling point of water is 100 degrees celsius. We present a replication with slightly different equipment leading to conclusions which confirm the earlier result". The accumulation of citations of a given paper is often a measure of its importance, and if the statement is eventually confirmed the pattern of citations will also serve to establish **priority**.

The construction of facts

What Latour has highlighted is the **pattern of progressive erosion, and eventual disappearance, of modalities as a statement becomes established as a fact in the sciences**. For instance, the next step might read as follows: "Numerous studies (Jones 2001, Smith 2002, Jones 2003, Bogdanoff 2010) have shown that the boiling point of water is around 100 degrees celsius, with minor variation; we show how this value depends on atmospheric pressure". Further still, one might read "it has been established that pure water boils at 100 degrees celsius; we investigate the effect of adjunction of various concentrations of salt in water".

At the endpoint of this process of acceptance of a fact, it becomes stripped of all modalities ("water boils at 100 degrees celsius"), but even more importantly it becomes operant in producing further knowledge, or technical effects instrumental in the production of knowledge: "to ensure a temperature of 100 degrees in our experiment we bring water to a boil". (For a more realistic example of this transformation happening to actual scientific facts, see Latour and Woolgar's Laboratory Life[14].)

Obviously, what makes this scheme of citations a process properly called scientific is its empirical and conversational character;

---

[14]http://en.wikipedia.org/wiki/Laboratory_Life

the erosion of modalities is not inexorable, a widely cited prelim-inary study may well be overturned by later work.

Another possibility is that the initial statement, the claimed "fact", never quite rids itself of all modalities. It remains spoiled by hedges and suspicions, and if no one can muster enough interest to follow it up in further publications, it may simply be forgotten. In the best case, that is - for in the worst case it may also persist in the collective discourse as **folklore**, myth or misconception[15].

The last chapter was a relatively informal application of these ideas, looking at the pattern of citations which led to the "cone of uncertainty" becoming entrenched as empirically supported fact, even though it started out as purely subjective. In the next two chapters we turn to another "well-known fact" of software engineering, and grapple more extensively with the role of citation.

 Key points

Many popularizers of ideas in software engineer-ing use citations in the style (Bossavit 2013) to lend their writings an air of authority. It is often merely a rhetorical device, and learning not to be fooled is an important addition to your critical thinking toolkit.

However, keep in mind that citations play an important part in science and scientific writing, not only as acknowledgment of previous work but also as an integral part of science's incremental character.

---

[15]http://en.wikipedia.org/wiki/List_of_common_misconceptions#Science

Chapter 5: The hunt for the 10x files

You have perhaps come across something like the following statement: "numerous studies have found 10:1 differences in productivity among individual programmers". Let's call this, for short, the "10x claim".

This is a book about the software profession's leprechauns, not a mystery novel, so I won't keep you in suspense about the conclusions I reached when I researched the issue: the 10x claim is poorly supported by empirical evidence; that is, essentially anecdotal. It persists largely because we lack any well-articulated theory of what productivity consists of for a programmer.

Why is this important? Isn't it obvious?

Several people questioned the value of investigating the claim, on the basis that "obviously" there are large differences in productivity among programmers, based on everyday experience or analogy with other human endeavors such as running marathons or writing symphonies, and therefore that no "studies" or precise measurements are required to prove it.

I do not dispute that there are large variations in *reported measurements* of programmer productivity; however, close examination of the evidence suggests that this observed variability originates in vague definitions of the term, in unreliable instruments of measurement, or in uncontrolled environmental factors, much more than it does in the intrinsic capabilities of programmers at comparable levels of training and experience.

There are many claims which have surface plausibility and turn out wrong, such as the "well-known fact" that you shouldn't go for a swim within an hour of eating. There are many claims which not only have surface plausibility but also appear to be borne out by everyday experience; a good example is the "well-known fact" that we use only a small fraction of the brain cells we are born with.

Many things of this order are both "obvious" and dead wrong.

A number of people believe that equally obviously we are quite ignorant of what makes a programmer productive. Everyday experience is no substitute for the critical examination of claims, for taking a close look at the research and the evidence, and using our entire brains to understand what this research tells us about programmers and the measurement of programmers.

Another benefit of this examination of the evidence for the 10x claim is that it offers an opportunity to look back on the short but fascinating history of the software engineering discipline, and to see what kind of conversations software engineering research consists of. The rest of this chapter is for curious people, who do not take "move along, nothing to see here" for an answer.

The impressive list of references

The 10x claims has been around forever - at least if you define "forever" as "since the beginnings of software engineering as an academic discipline", and then we have a perfect match in the year 1968, as we'll shortly see.

The list of references most often seen (in secondary citations, that is, usually from people who have read none of the papers) comes from an article originally published on Steve McConnell's blog, and reprinted in edited form as a chapter in the O'Reilly book "Making Software" (McConnell 2010).

These references are: Sackman et al. 1968, Curtis 1981, Mills 1983, DeMarco and Lister 1985, Curtis et al. 1986, Card 1987, Boehm and Papaccio 1988, Valett and McGarry 1989, Boehm et al 2000.

Their sheer number - 9 references in total - appears to lend significant weight to the 10x claim. But how strong, really, is the empirical support conferred to the 10x claim by the above list of references?

The original study and the 10x claim

"Sackman et al. 1968" is generally considered the original study - the one that started the ball rolling. It characterizes the experiments reported on as follows: "exploratory experiments (...) to compare debugging performance of programmers working under conditions of online and offline access to a computer".

To put things in historical context, 1968 was also the year of the NATO conference which saw the birth of "software engineering" as a topic of study and research. People active in this newborn discipline saw a need to point to research accomplishments to justify its status.

Here is the main result from the study:

...faster debugging under online conditions, but perhaps the most important practical finding involves
the striking individual differences in programmer
performance.

This is reported, in Table III, as a ratio of 28:1 between best and
worst times for one of the debugging tasks, **a figure still quoted
uncritically in some contemporary texts and media** (Mall,
Huang). They summarize the finding somewhat whimsically in
the text, without reference to the specific 28:1 ratio, but by
quoting a nursery rhyme: "When a programmer is good, he is
very, very good, but when he is bad, he is horrid."

Just so we're clear on what the 10x claim *is*, I'll quote the
following passage:

when programmers are first exposed to (...) computers, a general factor of programming proficiency is
held to account for a large proportion of observed
individual differences.

The claim, then, is that some unknown factor (or set of factors)
intrinsic to the programmer (rather than, say, environmental
conditions) has a variability that translates into the bulk of the
"observed individual differences". The whole range of this factor
is estimated, summarizing several distinct measurements, as an
"order of magnitude" ratio between best and worst performance.

Harshly criticized

The original study came under harsh criticism as soon as it came
out. (To be perfectly accurate, the "real" original is Sackman and

Grant 1967 rather than Sackman et al. 1968 - see full references at the end of Appendix A. The differences are minute, but the former really deserves to be called the "original" study.)

The 1967 paper was followed in the same journal by a scathing critique by Butler Lampson; a choice quote: "Perusal of the paper leaves a strong impression that the authors are not in close touch with reality." (It isn't unusual for journal editors to publish both a paper and a response to it when they know that such a paper is going to be controversial.)

Surveying the literature in 1981, thirteen years after the pilot experiment, an article by Thomas Dickey in *Proceedings of the IEEE* wryly noted of the Sackman experiment that "this single source, by means of different paths, is responsible for a large percentage of the common stock of 'knowledge' that programming productivity is totally unpredictable". Worse, added Dickey, **Sackman's stats didn't check out.**

Dickey pointed out that the 28:1 ratio was observed because "subject 7 required 170 hours to program the 'algebra' program in a batch environment, in machine language (while) subject 3 required 6 hours to program the same problem in JTS (ALGOL) in a time-shared environment."

Sackman shouldn't have directly compared the best and worst performances in the entire set, argued Dickey, but rather the best and worst among programmers placed by the experimental setup under comparable conditions.

Dickey concludes: "After accounting for the differences in the classes, only a range of 5:1 can be attributed to programmer variability." By then it was too late, of course, to put the genie back into the bottle, the claim was already widely circulated, and

Dickey even pointed to a specific article: "The Mongolian Hordes Versus Superprogrammer" (J. L. Ogdin, Infosystems, December 1973), as the origin of the popularization of the claim, its vehicle out of academia and into the broader culture of programming.

The title of that article, acknowledged by historians of the field as pivotal in bringing the "software engineering" debate to the attention of the business community, gives us another perspective on the 10x claim: its importance as a polarizing trope in the debates on the management of programmers, debates which are still raging today.

The 10x files

Obviously, the story didn't stop with Dickey. Someone who likes leprechauns will argue that even if Sackman wasn't right, we're still left with (take a deep breath) Curtis 1981, Mills 1983, DeMarco and Lister 1985, Curtis et al. 1986, Card 1987, Boehm and Papaccio 1988, Valett and McGarry 1989 and Boehm et al 2000.

Surely so many authors can't all be wrong? Wouldn't it be futile to systematically go through that list and check for the data?

Let me try to convince you that it is *not* futile, by showing you the result of that systematic analysis in a format which I hope is more useful than the above "wall o' cites".

Supporting sources for 10x, table 1

Reference	Direct?	Task type	Sample size
Curtis 1981	Y/N	Debugging	27
Mills 1983	Y	unknown	unknown
DeMarco and Lister 1985	Y	program to spec	166
Curtis et al. 1986	N	n/a	n/a
Card 1987	N	project	unknown
Boehm and Papaccio 1988	N	n/a	n/a
Valett and McGarry 1989	N	project	150
Boehm 2000	Y	project	161 (projects)

Supporting sources for 10x, table 2

Reference	Population	Measure	Effect studied	Variation
Curtis 1981	pros	time-to-complete	LOC on debug time	22:1 and 8:1
Mills 1983	unknown	unknown	unknown	10:1
DeMarco and Lister 1985	pros	time-to-complete	workplace	5.6:1

Supporting sources for 10x, table 2

Reference	Population	Measure	Effect studied	Variation
Curtis et al. 1986	n/a	n/a	n/a	various
Card 1987	pros	LOC per staff hour	none	not claimed*
Boehm and Pa-paccio 1988	n/a	n/a	n/a	various
Valett and Mc-Garry 1989	pros	LOC per staff hour	none	not claimed*
Boehm 2000	pros	manager's evalua-tion	none	not claimed

* - see discussion below; a textual claim of "6 or 10 to 1" is found in the primary

Good study, bad study

When presented with empirical evidence, you'll usually want to ascertain its quality. For instance, an experiment is more convincing from a statistical point of view (all other things equal) if it has a larger sample size.

Another important question is whether all the studies are talking about the same thing, which is why the tables above note which kind of task was being studied and what kind of effect was reported.

Also, you want to be sure that the results from a study are generalizable to "the real world". Students are commonly used as study subjects because researchers typically have ready access to students at affordable cost ("convenience samples"). However this can lead to distortions of the results, if there are systematic differences between students and professionals which can bias observations; for instance for our purpose, if the performance of students can be expected to be more variable than that of professional programmers.

Sometimes it's not even possible to answer the questions above, because the reference you're pointed to is a *secondary* source, that is, a paper which discusses some earlier study. That's kind of a big deal if **you want your degree of belief to be determined by the quantity and quality of the empirical evidence**, rather than by the number of apparently authoritative assertions of the claim; you want to guard against any double-counting of data sets, for instance.

The wild goose chase

One thing jumps out from the table above: most of the sources in McConnell's list are secondary, and provide no direct information on the empirical data or the methodology for its collection. They're useless for fact-checking!

Since I *really* wanted to know how much store I ought to put in the 10x claim, I was left with no choice but to chase down the primary sources. This was an incredibly tortuous process, as the "telephone game" pattern manifested time and again in the way the newer papers cited older papers which in turn cited still older ones... Rather than put you to sleep with a blow-by-blow analysis (which I reproduce in Appendix A for the terminally curious), I'll end this chapter with a quick summary of all the primary sources I was able to identify with discernible empirical data:

- Boehm, Brown and Lipow, 1973
- Sheppard et al. 1979
- Curtis 1981
- McGarry 1982
- DeMarco and Lister 1985

The "Mills 1983" reference, which I'll examine more closely in the next chapter, does not directly mention or indirectly reference empirical data. Two references, Boehm 1981 and Boehm 2000, *do* constitute a treatment of empirical data, but as we'll see in the next chapter this data is **not relevant to the 10x claim for individuals**.

Note that *only one* of these sources (DeMarco and Lister 1985) is from the original list of 8 sources claimed to confirm the original study. The list looks almost nothing like the original!

To my eyes at least, the original list of references has taken on the look of a smokescreen: it exaggerates both the number and the period of time spanned by the actual studies, and anyone who's really intent on looking up the raw factual data behind the claim is in for a long and frustrating search.

This is problematic enough... but if you can bear with me for a *second* chapter devoted to the 10x claim, we'll see that the "supporting" data isn't even all that supportive!

Key points

We want our degree of belief in a claim to be determined by the quantity and quality of the empirical evidence, rather than by irrelevant factors such as the claim's popularity.

Because research work is often reported poorly or falsely, it is important to look for the **primary** source rather than secondary or indirect reports.

Alas, even in the Google Age where all information, especially scientific, should be at everyone's fingertips, it often takes a lot of work to locate primary sources. Yet, there is no substitute for reading the real thing.

References

(McConnell 2010) "What Does 10x Mean? Measuring Variations in Programmer Productivity", in "Making Software", O'Reilly, 2010, p567

(Mall) Fundamentals of Software Engineering, Rajib Mall, Prentice-Hall of India, 2004

(Huang) http://www2.cs.uh.edu/~jhuang/JCH/SE/estimation.ppt (retrieved 27/01/2011)

(Sheppard et al. 1979) S. B. Sheppard, B. Curtis, P. Milliman, and T. Love, "Modern coding practices and programmer performance," Comput., vol. 12, no. 12, pp. 41-49, 1979

(McGarry 1982) F. E. McGarry, "What have we learned in the last six years?" in Proc. 7th Annu. Software Engineering Workshop (SEL-82-007) (Greenbelt, MD: NASA Coddard Space Flight Center), 1982.

(Brown and Lipow 1973) Brown, J. R., and M. Lipow, The quantitative Measurement of Software Safety and Reliability, revised from TRW Report No. SDP-1776, August 1973, TRW Software

(Curtis 1981) Curtis, Bill. 1981. "Substantiating Programmer Variability." Proceedings of the IEEE 69, no. 7: 846.

(DeMarco and Lister 1985) DeMarco, Tom, and Timothy Lister. 1985. "Programmer Performance and the Effects of the Workplace." Proceedings of the 8th International Conference on Software Engineering. Washington, D.C.: IEEE Computer Society Press, 268-72.

Chapter 6: The variable programmer

At the end of the previous chapter, we reached our pot of gold at the end of the rainbow, despite many obstacles in our path: actual research!

But how good *really* is the research claimed to support the 10x claim?

Getting just the results you want

Let's start by looking at the 1973 study by Brown and Lipow: "The quantitative Measurement of Software Safety and Reliability". (What I can say about it actually comes from a fairly detailed secondary report in Boehm, Brown and Lipow, 1976; the original paper proved too hard to track down.)

The authors give the following account of the experiment:

> there was a deliberate difference in quality emphasis in the two programming efforts: one was done by a 'hotshot' programmer who was encouraged to maximize code efficiency, and one by a careful programmer who was encouraged to emphasize simplicity (...) The main results of the study were: ten times as many errors were detected in the 'efficient' program.

In other words, *the reported 10:1 disparity can most economically be explained by the experimenters' selection of subject and instructions to focus on different objectives.* (This is consistent with a similar experiment by Weinberg and Schulman: when you ask programmers to focus on some objective among efficiency, quality, etc., they reliably produce output that maximizes that objective, at the sacrifice of all others.) No conclusion can be drawn regarding the variance between programmers in comparable conditions.

Boehm and Papaccio's interpretation fifteen years later, attributing the disparity to "differences between people", is totally at odds with this straightforward reading of the experimental setup; we can speculate that time and forgetting are to blame.

Within-subject variability

In the same 1981 volume of *Proceedings of the IEEE* where Dickey pointed out serious flaws in the Sackman study, the editors published a brief response by Bill Curtis, who in defense of the "variability" thesis discussed an earlier study, Sheppard et al. 1979. Curtis was, it turns out, one of the "et al".

The study, titled "Modern coding practices and programmer performance", examined three kinds of tasks: debugging, program comprehension and program modification. In his response to Dickey, Curtis singled out for discussion data obtained from a "pre-test" of the study (thus not "really" experimental data), and specifically from the debugging task.

Debugging is known as an open-ended sort of activity, and even seasoned programmers expect variable completion times when faced with this type of task. We do not know how well findings regarding debugging may generalize to programming overall.

The authors of the actual study, in the section "Differences among programmers", made no claims regarding best-to-worst ratios. They did note that experience did not generally correlate with performance in any of the three experiments.

But here is the important part. In the 1981 paper, Curtis went on to say: "with continued experience on the task **the programmer who spent 67 minutes on our pretest improved his performance substantially** during later experimental trials".

This suggests that there is an important "within-subject" variability, **an observation which undermines the 10x claim.** (Suppose we were to measure how many times you smile in a day. We might find that some days you smile only once, and other days you smile ten times or more. If we ran this same experiment on several subjects very similar to you, we would find a ratio of 10:1, but we would be wrong to conclude that "the happiest people smile ten times as often as the unhappiest": variability in what is being measured accounts, in this thought experiment, for *all* of the ratio between high and low measurements.)

Rocket science: the NASA data

Possibly the best data set from the list is that resulting from the work at NASA's Software Engineering Laboratory, leading to the publication of McGarry 1982, "What have we learned in the past six years?".

This includes data from 46 projects, all in the domain of "flight dynamic related software systems", and a total population of 150 "programmers and managers". The NASA SEL data does appear to directly support the 10x claim, and in fact the authors make this claim in as many words.

The method for collecting data was to have programmers fill out weekly forms, "attributing their time to the activity that they felt they were actually doing, no matter what phase of software development they were in". The text does not precisely explain how the component measurements ("LOC attributed to person" and "hours of effort attributed to person") were derived from the weekly forms, cites no threats to validity, and does not break out the data in any form closer to raw.

The text also provides no way to evaluate whether the various individuals assessed were working under roughly comparable conditions, or whether environmental rather than individual differences could account for the variation observed: for instance, working in low-level versus high-level programming languages, or workspace conditions (as we encounter in the discussion of DeMarco and Lister, below).

The separation of the data into "large project" and "small project", with markedly different ratios in the two cases, presents a puzzle. If what was measured was the difference between programmers rather than some environmental influence, so that by hypothesis the "large" versus "small" contexts had no effect, how do we explain the difference between the values? The authors offer this explanation:

> As has been found by other researchers in varying environments, the productivity of different programmers can easily differ by a factor of 6 or 10 to 1.

The SEL did find that there was a greater variation (from very low productivity of .5 LOC/hour to 10.8 LOC/hour) in small projects. The probable reason for this is that newer people are typically put on smaller projects and **the SEL has found extreme differences in the relatively inexperienced personnel.**

(A different kind of answer is that "best-to-worst ratio" may simply not be an adequate descriptor of the kind of probability distributions we are interested in, as opposed to the mean (which is fairly consistent between the large- and small-project populations) or the standard deviation (not reported by the authors). The best-to-worst ratio is very sensitive to variations at the extremes, which by their nature reflect only a small fraction of the overall population.)

Needle in a haystack

Let's take a brief look at "Mills 1983", which is in fact a reference to an entire book: Harlan Mills' "Software Productivity". At least the title is relevant!

This is a *great* illustration of one of my pet peeves with the "terse" citation style. Want to irritate a fact-checker? Give them a reference to a book of a few hundred pages *without* including a page or a section number, forcing them to go through the book with a fine-toothed comb.

Here is the only quote in the Mills book that is germane to the 10x claim - it appears on page 265:

There is a 10 to 1 difference in productivity among
practicing programmers today - that is, among programmers certified by their industrial position and
pay. That differential is undisputed, and it is a
sobering commentary on our ability to mesure and
enforce productivity standards in the industry.

That's it; that's all Mills wrote on the topic. Chronologically, it is
possible that Mills is referring to the NASA SEL data; or he may
be referring to his own experience at IBM as "the" original Chief
Programmer. The "Chief Programmer Team" was a technique
invented by Mills and extensively used at NASA - it involved a
"superprogrammer" bossing around a group of lesser individuals,
much as surgical teams are organized around a chief surgeon.

Incidentally, it is worth observing that depending on the details
of data collection, the Chief Programmer Team concept in practice may be a *cause* of significant observed performance variations, since it would involve teaming up one high-performing
programmer with a few lesser ones.

However, Mills cites no sources, not even his own work, and as
far as I was able to ascertain, in the entire text of Mills' book **fails
to provide a smidgen evidential support for the 10x claim.**

The COCOMO haystacks

The same "needle in a haystack" problem applies to the two books
by Boehm. These references are quite burdensome to check, as
they do not give a page number (and as well as being expensive,
the books are quite effective as doorstops: lots of pages!)

These two books are the authoritative works on the COCOMO method of cost estimation, and its later update COCOMO II. The COCOMO model is an interesting tool and there are many who swear by it, but it is out of scope for this report to affirm or criticize the model. All that is relevant here is the empirical data. The COCOMO frameworks was synthesized from a historical data base. The reader interested in the raw data from the COCOMO studies can find most of it online (PROMISE 1981, PROMISE 2000). However, these studies concerned *projects* and not *individuals*.

Given the premise of this report, this is a critical issue. Only if they measured individuals could these references provide support for the form of the 10x claim that is the subject at hand, i.e. provide "confirmation" of the Sackman et al. experiment.

Page 47 of the 2000 book is explicit on this point, in its discussion of *PCAP*, the "cost driver" of the model representing "programmer capability": its measurement "**should be based on the capability of the programmers as a team rather than as individuals**".

Boehm's 1981 book, an older but in many respects more interesting work, offers no better support. McConnell has attempted to justify the relevance of the COCOMO data to the *individual* form of 10x by arguing that it "shows differences in team productivity based on programmer capability of 4.18 to 1. This is not quite an order of magnitude, but it is for teams, rather than for individuals".

The problem is that we *cannot infer* variations in individual productivity from data collected at the team level: **we do not have an adequate theory of how a team's productivity results**

from the aggregation of individual abilities, and in particular
we cannot assume that a team's output is a linear sum of
individual "productivities".

It's a common observation that a single toxic individual is
sometimes sufficient to destroy an entire team's performance,
and the reverse phenomenon of "catalyst" individuals is also
observed anecdotally. Teams are seen as a desirable manner of
organizing software development efforts precisely because of
such synergistic effects.

Environmental effects

The final data set that we'll look at, from DeMarco and Lister's 1985 article, describes the authors' "Coding War Games",
a competition in which contestants participated at their usual
workplace and during normal business hours. Contestants were
paired off, competing against each other as well as with other
pairs.

The text makes clear that this study took place under loosely
controlled conditions, for instance, in showing a "typical" time-
sheet recorded during the exercise, where one programmer was
interrupted no less than six times during a thirty-minute period
while taking part in the contest.

The authors report a 5.6:1 ratio between best and worst con-
tenders.

DeMarco and Lister however **disclaim the ascription of variability solely to individual programmer ability** : "While there
were wide variations across the sample, we found evidence that

characteristics of the workplace and of the organization seemed to explain a significant part of the difference."

They observe a variation of 1.2:1 within an average pair. It's unclear whether we can make any reliable inferences, based on what data the authors have made available, concerning the variability among individual programmers which *isn't* affected by environmental factors. It's within the realm of possibility that the best programmers worked in the worst environments, and that if we could adjust for these effects we would recover 10x differences, but there's no way to tell from the data presented.

We don't know in which direction to adjust the 5.6:1 ratio, given that it results in "significant part" from environmental factors. The best we can say is that the DeMarco and Lister study turns out, on closer examination, to have little to do with assessing variability in individual performance.

Summing up

How strong is the support conferred to the 10x claim by the best-reputed list of references, for a reader persistent enough to follow the chain of citations back to primary sources?

Based on our close reading of the "10x files", we can now answer: quite weak.

Not a single one of the references is to a replication, in the scientific sense of the term, of the original exploratory experiment.

The empirical data is in general quite old, most if not all of it predating widespread use of the Internet - which we can safely expect to have wrought major changes in programming practice.

None of the studies address the question of construct validity, that is, how meaningful it is to speak of an individual programmer's productivity, and if it is meaningful, whether the experimental measurements line up adequately with that meaning. (The persistent tendency of the software engineering community to underemphasize construct validity has been noted in Kaner's 2004 article, "Software Engineering Metrics: What Do They Measure and How Do We Know?".)

The 10x claim is "not even wrong", and the question of "how variable is individual programmer productivity" should be dissolved rather than answered.

 Key points

Just citing a publication of some kind as support for a claim is not enough to compel belief in the claim. The source itself has to be examined critically.

Often, what is cited is only opinion, or work of dubious status. A great many things should count as "evidence": quantitative but also qualitative research, experience reports, and so on; but just saying "this is so" or "someone else has proved it" doesn't count.

Finally, even when the source is a true account of research, it may not support the author's claim, or it could be too inconclusive to have much influence on our beliefs.

References

PROMISE 1981[16] (last checked 28/06/2015)

PROMISE 2000[17] (last checked 28/06/2015)

Kaner 2004[18] (last checked 28/06/2015)

---

[16]http://openscience.us/repo/effort/cocomo/coc81.html
[17]http://openscience.us/repo/effort/cocomo/nasa93.html
[18]http://www.kaner.com/pdfs/metrics2004.pdf

Interlude: How To Lie

Chapter 7: Who's afraid of the Big Bad Waterfall?

Let's take a break from the numbers game for a chapter or two, and examine some qualitative rather than quantitative claims. They're fun too! And we'll get back to "harder" topics quite soon. We are, however, still looking at how strong opinions can form around a topic, quite independently of any evidence that exists on the topic.

As software professionals, we should be interested in knowing at least the basics of our own history, for just the same reasons that as citizens we are expected to know about our national history and about world history: so that we will be able to make informed decisions and know who to trust, who to listen to; so that we are not deceived by lies. Untrue histories generally have an agenda - "someone trying to sell you something", as the saying goes.

Quite a bit of the current debate on software engineering relies on opinions regarding the "creation myth" of the discipline: the so-called waterfall model of sequential software development, also known as the SDLC (Software Development Life Cycle).

Unfortunately, most of these opinions are wildly inaccurate.

The standard story

An article[19] by Robert Martin provides (along with some other interpretations that I'll come back to) what is now the nearly universal explanation of how conceptions of the SDLC became pervasive in the discourse of software engineering:

> In 1970 a software engineer named Dr. Winston W. Royce wrote a seminal paper entitled Managing the Development of Large Software Systems. This paper described the software process that Royce felt was appropriate for large-scale systems. As a designer for the Aerospace industry, he was uniquely qualified. [...] Royce's paper was an instant hit. It was cited in many other papers, including several very important process documents in the early '70s. One of the most influential of these was DOD2167, the document that described the software development process for the American Department of Defense. Royce was acclaimed, and became known as the father of the DOD process.

You can find further confirmation of the "seminal" character of Royce's paper on Wikipedia:

> The first formal description of the waterfall model is often cited as a 1970 article by Winston W. Royce, though Royce did not use the term "waterfall" in this article.

---

[19]http://cleancoder.posterous.com/what-killed-waterfall-could-kill-agile

For many, the standard story is the whole story; over the ensuing decades, even though many variants on the "waterfall" life cycle were proposed that all have their uses in one context or another, the waterfall still remains one of the major foundations of software engineering. It's the model to learn as a basis for learning other variants, and as such is taught quite seriously at many universities. It is a constant fallback of enterprise software development efforts, a norm against which other models are judged.

In any case, the following are widely, in fact almost universally, agreed upon:

- Dr. Winston Royce "invented" the waterfall model in 1970
- The nascent software engineering community welcomed the break from "artisanal" practice of the past
- The model was instantly enthusiastically adopted as a sequential, non-overlapping phases model
- Having become an industry norm, the model was taken up by the US DoD
- Variants of the model were developed later and used where appropriate

Alternate endings

There are at least two "modern" endings to the mythical story, told by different people according to whether they agree with the tenets of the Agile movement; for the Agilists,

- Tragically, this was all a misunderstanding, based on careless reading of Royce

- Royce was actually advocating an "iterative and incremental" approach in his paper (!)

Whereas for people who disagree with Agilists,

- "waterfall" is recent coinage and has been used only as a straw-man term
- formal lifecycles are not actually as inflexible and risky as "waterfall" is made out to be
- Royce's paper wasn't actually advocating a rigid sequential approach

The article by Robert Martin cited above is representative of the first group, which I'm tempted to characterize as "agile revisionists"; for instance he writes:

> [Royce] began the paper by setting up a straw-man process to knock down. He described this naïve process as "grandiose". He depicted it with a simple diagram on an early page of his paper. Then the paper methodically tears this "grandiose" process apart. [...] Apparently the authors of DOD2167 did not actually read Royce's paper; because they adopted the "grandiose", naïve process that Royce's paper had derided. To his great chagrin, Dr. Winston W. Royce became known as the father of the waterfall.

Larman and Basili, in their "Brief History" of iterative and incremental development, offer support this interpretation with a quote by Walker Royce - the son of Winston Royce: "He was always a proponent of iterative, incremental, evolutionary development."

The second group is well represented by the following excerpts from a 2003 Web essay, titled "There's no such thing as the Waterfall Approach (and there never was)":

> I don't recall when I first saw that term, but I'm sure it was in a pejorative sense. I'm unaware of any article or paper that ever put forth the "waterfall methodology" as a positive or recommended approach to system development. In fact, "waterfall" is a straw-man term, coined and used by those trying to promote some new methodology by contrasting it with a silly alleged traditional approach that no competent methodology expert ever favored. [...] Phase disciplines, when practiced with sensible judgment and flexibility, are a good thing with no offsetting downside. They are essential to the success of large projects. Bogus attacks on the non-existent "waterfall approach" can obscure a new methodology's failure to support long-established sensible practice.

Just the facts

In fact, *both* modern interpretations are demonstrably wrong. Not only that - but *all* the elements of the standard myth turn out to be false or at least substantially at odds with the historical record.

First, what was Royce actually saying in that 1970 paper? Many who echo the "agile revisionist" quote a part of that paper where he says that the unmodified sequential approach "is risky and invites failure".

However, as we all know, with selective quotation we can make anyone say anything we want. The full sentence was "I believe in this concept, but the implementation described above is risky and invites failure." In other words, Royce is cautioning against simplistic interpretations, but not condemning the basic idea; a few paragraph further Royce adds this, which for some reason is much more rarely quoted:

> I believe the illustrated approach to be fundamentally sound. The remainder of this discussion presents five additional features that must be added to this basic approach to eliminate most of the development risks.

From a close reading of Royce's paper, "the illustrated approach" refers to Figure 3; that is, the picture showing a "cascading" series of activities, but allowing that iteration occurs between succeeding phases (the analysis phase may undergo rework on the basis of errors uncovered in the design phase, for instance; or the design may undergo rework as a result of errors in the coding phase). The "risky and invites failure" comment can be inferred, from its placement in the text, to refer to Figure 2 - which showed the same cascade of activities but no feedback loops at all.

Regarding the "five additional features", again many people give in to the temptation to mention only one, that supports their reinterpretation of Royce: the recommendation to "Do It Twice", i.e. flush out technical risk by building a prototype; and this is only #3 of the five. For completeness, the remaining four recommended features are:

- add what we would now call an "architecture phase" at the start of the process (#1)
- err on the side of too much documentation (#2)
- make sure to "plan, control and monitor" the testing process (#4)
- have the customer formally involved to sign off on various deliverables (#5)

Finally, Royce's "iterative" recommendations stop short of allowing at any point that the first two "requirements" phases of the cycle can be included within an iterative loop: the "Do It Twice" recommendation is confined to the design and implementation stages.

No paper is an island

Anyone with an interest in so-called "development processes" should read the Royce paper carefully at least a couple times in their careers, but the really interesting part comes when we remember that in any discipline with an academic tradition, papers don't exist in isolation.

Fortunately, with the help of today's Web serious bibliographic research is within everyone's reach. For instance, we can use Google Scholar to understand the real history of Royce's paper within the larger context of the software engineering discipline.

Scholar gives us in particular a list of the *citations* of Royce's paper, which can be narrowed by date.

Did Royce's 1970 paper "invent" or "formally define for the first time" the concept of the software development life cycle, or the notion of a succession of stages?

The answer is no: the first papers cited that mention (and draw a diagram of) a sequential or stagewise model of software development go back at least to 1956. The identification of Royce's paper as the origin of the waterfall is largely arbitrary. Royce's paper *was* however the origin of the most common *picture* of the waterfall - with its instantly recognizable downward cascade of boxes (and the loops showing iteration between phases, which some later authors omit). But as I'll explain presently, that was probably not Royce's fault at all - though it wasn't due to careless reading either.

Was Royce's paper "an instant hit"? The answer is no.

Taking a step back, let's look at a graphical representation of how often Royce's paper is cited in the software engineering literature:

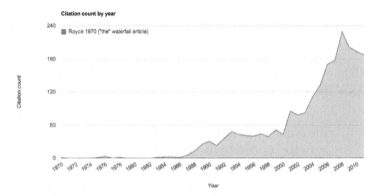

Figure 1

We can see that the 1970 paper in fact remained almost totally unknown until 1987.

What the chart doesn't show is a peculiar property of these early citations: just about every single one of them is by an author at TRW, a US defense contractor who employed several of the authors involved in the early years of the software engineering discipline, including Barry Boehm, known for an exceptional number of contributions to the field.

It turns out that Boehm (who cannot be accused of having read Royce "carelessly") used Royce's well-known diagram (Figure 3, the one with feedback loop between successive phases that Royce characterized as "fundamentally sound") in a 1976 paper modestly titled "Software Engineering".

In that paper, Boehm didn't give credit to Royce for the picture (though he cites an unrelated paper of Royce's). Rather, that diagram was used, with only the briefest of explanation, to provide a structure for the rest of the paper, which examined phase by phase the recent advances in software engineering. Several early authors in fact refer to the diagram as "Boehm's waterfall", rather than "Royce's waterfall".

Here is a quote from a paper by two of Boehm's colleagues at TRW the same year:

> The evolution of approaches for the development of software systems has generally paralleled the evolution of ideas for the implementation of code. Over the last ten years more structure and discipline have been adopted, and practicioners have concluded that a top-down approach is superior to the bottom-up approach of the past. The Military Standard set MIL-STD 490/483 recognized this newer approach [...] The same top-down approach to a series of requirements statements is explained, without the specialized military jargon, in an excellent paper by Royce; he introduced the concept of the "waterfall" of development activities.

Rather than support the idea that Royce's paper drew instant support and influenced military practice in software development, this quote suggests quite the opposite: the defense contractor TRW (who also had contacts within the US Defense departments responsible at the time for defining these standards) seems to have seized on Royce's paper as a good introduction and justification of existing practice.

Late bloomer

Using Google Scholar to reconstruct the history of Royce's paper, we can finally better understand how it ended up being known as "the origin of waterfall".

Notice that there is a sudden surge of publications citing Royce's paper in 1987: this is due to the paper having been republished in that year's international software engineering conference, at the initiative of none other than Barry Boehm in his "Software Process Management: Lessons Learned from History[20]". Royce's paper was republished alongside two others that Boehm deemed of particular interest from a historical standpoint (one of the others was the 1956 paper which already defined a stagewise model).

(Another sudden surge of publications can be seen around 2001: the cause is harder to identify, because by then the myth is well established and the overall number of papers published each year that cite Royce is quite significant; but it is a safe bet that this renewed interest is due to the growing popularity of Agile at that time.)

There was a very good reason to call attention to the waterfall model at that time: Boehm had just introduced the (iterative) Spiral model of software development which would become one of his most significant publications. Boehm wrote in 1987

> Royce's paper already incorporates prototyping as an essential step compatible with the waterfall model.

[20]http://dl.acm.org/citation.cfm?id=41798

Birth of a myth

What I find particularly striking in this quote is the "compatible with". Boehm seems to forget that if he takes Royce as the originator of waterfall then this prototyping step isn't *compatible with* waterfall - it is * part of* waterfall. So, in effect, this quotation is kind of a smoking gun - it is the rhetorical moment where waterfall is being separated into two halves, one "stupid" waterfall and one "enlightened" reading. This later enlightened reading isn't given the name waterfall, perhaps because to do so would diminish the import of Boehm's own "Spiral" contribution.

In this sense, the interpretation of the waterfall as a "straw man" is not entirely false. But it isn't accurate, either, to say that waterfall was *always* a straw man - for the first two decades, nearly, it was discussed generally quite favorably - if only within a relatively small circle of authors.

The story that the written record seems to tell is that the "Royce invented Waterfall" was a convenient myth. Convenient because people could satisfy the requirement of garnishing their papers with a citation, and because it provided a (relatively protean) straw man of "older, more primitive" processes that the more modern "iterative" processes could be contrasted with. And a myth whose career began seventeen years after original publication, breaking a long spell of obscurity but also starting down the road to infamy.

I find this story, the true story of waterfall, much more interesting and enlightening than its caricatures.

Key points

Ideas have histories. They don't come into the world complete and of one piece. An idea's history is often more interesting and complex than we suspect.

Knowing (and researching) the history of your field is an important asset in critical thinking. It will protect you from common misconceptions.

Indexes like Google and Google Scholar provide great opportunities to reconstruct the history of particular ideas and concepts, providing everyone with basic tools of bibliometrics ("a set of methods to quantitatively analyze scientific and technological literature" as defined by Wikipedia).

Chapter 8: Software's perpetual crisis

Here is a claim I long believed to be true: "The Software Engineering conference was convened in response to rising recognition of the software crisis." This seems logical - first comes the problem, then comes the solution.

The problem with this claim is that it's about 180 degrees from the truth, if you give any credit to a comparative search for both phrases in Google's corpus of books:

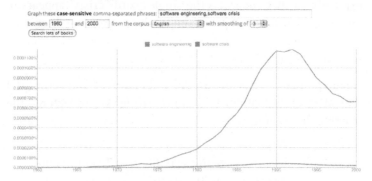

Comparative search

One is almost tempted to say, a little mischievously, that the software crisis is seen to result from software engineering, not the other way round. If you break out the two phrases separately, it's clear that the onset of popularity of "software engineering" coincides, as would be expected, with the 1968 NATO conference - though it really takes off in the mid-70s. The phrase "software crisis", on the other hand, lags well behind, at least by five years.

The solution came first, then a problem was defined to fit.

Thomas Haigh has written more extensively about the construction of the "crisis" trope, and it makes for a fascinating story:

http://tomandmaria.com/tom/Writing/SoftwareCrisis_SofiaDRAFT.pdf

One thing that you can easily verify, for instance, is that none of the participants quoted in the proceedings of the NATO conference *ever* refer to a "software crisis" by that name. The phrase "software crisis" appears exactly once in the proceedings, and that as an editorial comment. The same is true of the 1969 proceedings - neither of the *two* founding conferences referred explicitly to that concept. (The single word "crisis" appears in one section of the 1968 proceedings, alongside some discussion of the "software gap", which an editorial comment places on the same footing as the phrase "software crisis".)

Haigh points to Dijkstra as the originator of the term, and that successfully only in 1972 in his Turing Award lecture "The Humble Programmer[21]":

> Only a few years ago this was different: to talk about a software crisis was blasphemy. The turning point was the Conference on Software Engineering in Garmisch, October 1968, a conference that created a

---

[21]http://www.cs.utexas.edu/~EWD/transcriptions/EWD03xx/EWD340.html/

sensation as there occurred the first open admission of the software crisis.

Haigh suggests that it would be more accurate to say that "In 1972 a software crisis was proclaimed by Edsger Dijkstra to have been proclaimed in 1968 at the NATO Conference on Software Engineering."

 Key points

Just like "waterfall", the "software crisis" is more myth than reality, though an important part of the overall narrative that provides backdrop and justification for software engineering as a discipline as taught, researched and practiced.

Another freely available tool - Google's N-Gram "Lab" - provides us with additional ways to investigate the origin and spread of the "software crisis" meme and compare it to "software engineering".

Chapter 9: A Leprechaun hunting tutorial

I want to say a little bit about my methods. In the process, we'll unmask a new Leprechaun. We will also see that Leprechaun-hunting is easy - you can do it too. It's a matter of attitude.

Stemmatics[22], a branch of something called "textual criticism", is the study of text transmission. Here is a longer description, courtesy of Gregory Mayer:

> Stemmaticists carefully study texts, and attempt to determine which copies were made from which other copies. The copying is usually traced by the introduction of small copyist's errors, which are then perpetuated in any copies descended from the one in which the error arose. Tracing these small errors allows one to trace the history of the manuscripts.

This is basically what I do, using Google. Having a comprehensive index of nearly the entire Internet, reaching back very far back in history, that you can search in an instant - I don't know any stemmaticists personally, but Google strikes me as the Promised Land of stemmatics.

---

[22]http://www.canterburytalesproject.org/pubs/desc2.html

What I do is start with a claim that strikes me as dubious. Today I was looking over various instances of the "46% of features never used" claim (we'll get to this in a later chapter), and I noticed it was frequently accompanied by something like the following:

> The U.S. Department of Defense (DoD), when following a waterfall lifecycle, experienced a 75% failure rate.

(This is from one blog post[23] - there are many, many other citations to this work, "Jarzombek 1999".)

Exercise: find more citations, and note the context in which they occur.

My second reflex in such cases is to use the Google "search by date" feature to try and locate the earliest possible citation. In this case, I soon found a 2002 article[24] from CrossTalk, "The Journal of Defense Software Engineering".

Exercise: use the Google "search by date" feature yourself, using the search terms "Aerospace, Jarzombek, 1999" and try to replicate my results.

> At the 5th Annual Joint Aerospace Weapons Systems Support, Sensors, and Simulation Symposium in 1999, the results of a study of 1995 Department of Defense (DoD) software spending were presented. A summary of that study is shown in Figure 1. As

---

[23]http://techdistrict.kirkk.com/2010/02/10/agile-the-new-era/
[24]http://sunnyday.mit.edu/16.355/leishman.html

indicated, of $35.7 billion spent by the DoD for software, only 2 percent of the software was able to be used as delivered. The vast majority, 75 percent, of the software was either never used or was cancelled prior to delivery. The remaining 23 percent of the software was used following modification.

Now, of course $35.7Bn is a huge sum, and most certainly a representative sample. These numbers gave me pause.

My first reflex is to locate the original source - the cited text itself. On this occasion, though, as on many others, the original article is nowhere to be found. The "Joint Aerospace Weapons Systems Support, Sensors, and Simulation Symposium" or "JAWS S3" seems to have been "a thing", as the saying goes - but Google appears to have no trace of it.

Most people would give up there. As I said above, Leprechaun hunting is a matter of attitude. All you have to do is not give up, ever.

Exercise: (optional) - find the email address of one of the people citing Jarzombek; email them, politely and courteously asking if they still have a paper or electronic copy, and would mind sending you a PDF or a scan. This is an advanced practice. I have done this on several occasions, instead of giving up.

(Who did I email on this occasion? I chose to email the author, Lt. Col. Jarzombek (retired), directly. His reply: "I do not have readily available access to that information; yet Capers Jones (copied) would have similar data, and it would be more updated.")

Stemmatics to the rescue: my third reflex is to locate an important part of the claim and see if I can find an occurrence of that using Google.

Zeroing in on the pie chart in the CrossTalk article, I tried searching on the categories: for instance "Software used, but extensively reworked or abandoned" sounded promising.

Why? Because this phrase is a complex disjunction, unlikely to be independently reinvented by two authors. The expression "software used after changes", by comparison, could turn up in many places.

Exercise: try this Google search for yourself.

Unfortunately, searching for the full phrase turns up nothing new; the 2002 CrossTalk article, plus two later (2007 and 2009) copies.

Now can we finally give up? Of course not. We forge on. Stemmatics again: the original text is likely to have been somewhat distorted. This particular phrase still sounds promising, but we can try to take a guess at what it might have been distorted from.

Exercise: come up with your own variants on the phrase and Google them. Note your results.

My next move was to try dropping the "or abandoned". What I found filled me with shock and perverse joy. Googling for "software used but extensively reworked" leads among other things to a very enlightening publication[25]: a 1979 report by the "Comptroller General of the United States". It is a very official document, hosted on a legal documents website, quite unlikely to be a fake.

---

[25]http://bit.ly/XQWNCv

Page 11 is the smoking gun. It's a pie chart looking very much like the one in the 2002 article. The labels for the various categories match up almost exactly:

- "Software that could be used after changes" vs "Software used after changes"
- "Software that could be used as delivered" vs "Software used as delivered"
- "Software delivered but never successfully used" vs "Software delivered, but not successfully used"
- "Software used but extensively reworked or later abandoned" vs "Software used, but extensively reworked or abandoned"
- "Software delivered but never successfully used" - identical.
- "Software paid for but not delivered" - identical.

Stemmatics strongly suggests, even at this stage, that the (so far unseeen) 1995-1999 text is a copy, mutated, of the 1979 text.

Exercise: estimate the probability that the 1995-1999 text was independently written by a different author, but turned out (by coincidence, as it were) to use nearly the same phrasing.

What's more interesting even is the numbers. The GAO data was obtained as follows:

> We examined nine cases in detail, which included visits to both agency and contractor sites, examining documents, and interviewing those persons involved who could still be reached.

The total dollar amount of the projects involved was $6.8M - three orders of magnitude smaller than the $35.7Bn claimed for the 1995 study, even after adjusting for inflation.

Yet, the percentages match up almost exactly: - $119,000 out of $6,8M is 2% - $198,000 out of $6,8M is 3% - $3,2M out of $6,8M is 47% (compared to 46%) - $1,95M out of $6,8M is 29% - $1,3M out of $6,8M is 19% (compared to 20%)

Again, a quick probabilistic assessment: it is virtually impossible for a 1995 study on thirty billion dollars' worth of projects to turn up the exact same numbers (within 1% tolerance) as a 1979 study of seven million dollars' worth, totally independently - and also by coincidence use the exact same categories to classify projects.

(I ran my reasoning by a professional statistician. Her suggestion was to use a two-sided chi-squared test, taking for "unit of population" the cost of the smallest project known in the set, or $119M, and taking as a null hypothesis that the latter set of percentages results "by coincidence" from an independent sampling - as opposed to being a copy of the earlier one. This is of course a debatable set of assumptions, but in her professional judgment not unreasonable. Her calculation rules out the null with a p-value lower than 0.0001, that is, with a very high degree of confidence.)

Conclusion? Even though I have never seen, and probably will never see, the Jarzombek "study", I know it cannot be true.

This doesn't mean, by the way, that I'm accusing Stanley "Joe" Jarzombek of making stuff up: I couldn't say anything definite on that until I saw the original text. It seems at least equally plausible that someone who actually attended his presentation got their wires crossed, and somehow confused a 1995 survey on billions of dollars' worth of projects with the 1979 survey, perhaps cited by Jarzombek.

What matters is that the Jarzombek citation is a Leprechaun - totally bogus. Another one bites the dust.

Final exercise: replicate this search for a different claim that strikes you as potentially dubious.

An interesting coda: some of my searches turned up a close variant of the claim where the study is described as being of "a $37Bn sample of DoD projects". It turns out that the $37B is a late corruption; searching for one[26] then the other[27] reveals that the $37B appears in 2005. (That's only a $1.3 billion inaccuracy - small change, eh? - I wouldn't mind seeing that much in book sales, though.)

Interestingly enough, Googling for "$35.7 billion dod software costs" brings up an earlier result that looks like a very credible primary source: this 1994 document[28] saying in part:

> The MCCRMG[29] (Mission-Critical Computer Resources Management Guide) estimated that by 1995 DoD software costs will approach $35.7 billion, up from $11.4 billion in 1985.

There cannot have been, then, a "$35.7B **sample** of DoD projects" - that was the DoD's best projected estimate of the **total** size of its software costs in 1995. This is yet another strike against the

---

[26]http://bit.ly/YkgFek
[27]http://bit.ly/YkgIXn
[28]http://1.usa.gov/XSrsjw
[29]http://1.usa.gov/YkhaVD

original claim, but there's no point beating a dead horse - I have another reason to bring this up.

Why does the claim, as usually quoted, suggest that the $35.7B was a "sample"? Because that's the language of statistics, and the entire rhetoric of Leprechaun claims hinges on their looking like "proper" empirical investigation: studying a smaller sample of an overall population, and drawing inferences from sample mean to population mean

To understand this is to understand a big part of the entire Leprechaun phenomenon.

 Key points

Leprechaun-hunting requires little in the way of specialized tools or skills, but is rather a matter of attitude; tracking down the origins of claims is largely a matter of curiosity and tenacity.

Google's "search by date" feature proves invaluable in tracking the spread of particular phrases across time.

The fundamental insight of stemmatics is that minor errors or alterations afford tracing the "genealogical tree" of variations of an ancestor text. Combining this idea with "search by date" allows us to trace claims back to their point of origin.

Chapter 10: The cost of defects: an illustrated history

Everybody knows that the later you find defects, the more expensive it is to fix them... Unfortunately, it turns out that "everybody knows" it in more or less the same way "everybody knows" that the Great Wall of China is the only man-made structure visible from space to the naked eye.

That is, it's a claim that has some surface plausibility and has gained widespread acceptance, but turns out on closer examination to be not just awkwardly vague, but in fact almost entirely anecdotal.

Origins

Here is how the "curve" first appeared, in the "Software Requirements Engineering" section of Boehm's landmark 1976 article, which was titled straightforwardly (if perhaps a little immodestly) "Software Engineering".

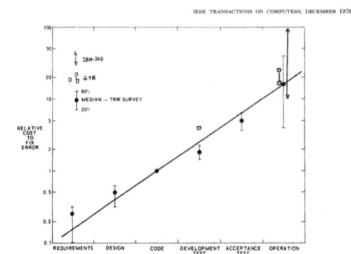

IEEE TRANSACTIONS ON COMPUTERS, DECEMBER 1976

Fig. 3.   Software validation: the price of procrastination.

First appearance of Boehm's curve

Note well the axes and their scales. The horizontal scale is discrete - even though the added diagonal suggests that it is continuous. It represents the successive phases of the "software development life cycle" (also known as the "waterfall").

The vertical scale represents a ratio of two numbers: the "relative cost" of fixing a defect that is detected in a given phase, as opposed to fixing the same defect in a different phase. The (arbitrary) origin or "baseline" of this comparison is fixed at the coding stage.

Note also that the scale is *logarithmic*: the straight line segment drawn through the various data points therefore means, "it gets exponentially more expensive to correct a defect, if you detect it later rather than earlier".

The article attempted to provide a definition of that phrase, survey current practice, and identify areas of future improvement. In this context, the diagram was intended to justify the "critical nature of software requirements engineering", explained as "the discipline for developing a complete, consistent, unambiguous specification - which can serve as a basis for common agreement among all parties concerned".

Boehm concluded from the diagram that "it pays off to invest effort in finding requirements errors early and correcting them in, say, 1 man-hour rather than waiting to find the error during operations and having to spend 100 man-hours correcting it". In other words, it was an economic rationale for a substantial requirements analysis effort ahead of any other activity.

First amendments

The initial version was cited a few times, but Boehm's big hit was the slightly different version presented in his hugely influential 1981 book, "Software Engineering Economics".

It is quite easy to find reproductions of the 1981 version with a Google search for the verbatim phrase, "phase in which error was detected and corrected". Here, for instance, is a reproduction from a 1992 document:

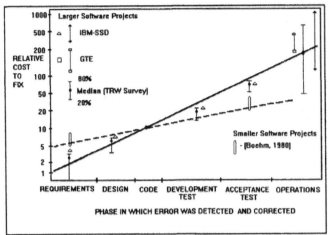

Figure 3. Increase in Cost-To-Fix or Change Software Throughout the Life Cycle (Boehm, 1981:40)

Later, common appearance of Boehm's curve

Note the first few of many changes, alterations and amendments to affect later versions of the curve.

In the 1981 version, a further exponential relationship is suggested, though with a smaller slope: this, Boehm suggests, only applies to "smaller projects". Another interesting thing is that four data points, supposedly from studies at IBM, have been added to the chart - even though Boehm's 1981 book references *exactly* the same IBM paper as his 1976 article. (Not pictured in the above diagram, but shown in the 1981 book, is data supposedly from the "Safeguard" project at Bell Labs.)

This 1981 version is the one that Boehm reproduces in his chapter of the 2010 book "Making Software", and so we can assume it is his preferred, "definitive" version. The rest of the profession, as we'll shortly see, had other ideas.

Where's the data?

As in our earlier stories about the Cone of Uncertainty and the "10X" claim, reading the primary sources in a search for the underlying evidence justifying Boehm's curve turns out to be a frustrating but in some ways enlightening exercise.

To summarize, the data just isn't up to any reasonable standard of "research". The longer version is given in Appendix B, for the curious reader; its inclusion here would bloat this chapter out of decent proportions, and in any case the really interesting story turns out to be how Boehm's curve gets increasingly distorted from the late 1990's onward. We will only look at some highlights.

The "smaller projects" curve turns out to be from only two teams of first-year students, a sample size so small that extrapolating to "smaller projects in general" is totally indefensible. The GTE study does not explain its data, other than to say it came from two projects, one large and one small. The paper cited for the Bell Labs "Safeguard" project specifically disclaims having collected the fine-grained data that Boehm's data points suggest. The IBM study (Fagan's paper) contains claims which seem to contradict Boehm's graph, and no numerical results which clearly correspond to his data points.

Boehm doesn't even cite a paper for the TRW data, except when writing for "Making Software" in 2010, and there he cited the original 1976 article. There exists a large study conducted at TRW at the right time for Boehm to cite it, but that paper doesn't contain the sort of data that would support Boehm's claims.

Metamorphoses

Authors until the late 1990's appear to have taken some pains to reproduce Boemh's original diagram fairly faithfully; but as the years pass, we begin to see the "Boehm curve" distorted in ever more creative ways. (The chronology is a little hazy, and while there are ways to pin it down a little more precisely, I hope you will forgive me for limiting my research to the bare minimum needed to show you the overall trends.)

Below, for instance, is an interesting version from 1996, changing the shape to a pyramid. But this is an oddity; the pyramid is nice-looking but not at all a good fit to the type of data being represented.

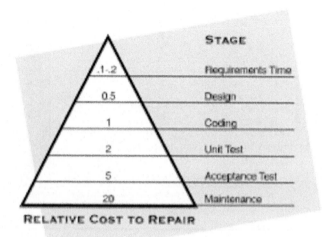

Simplified Boehm's curve - pyramid

Two more "mainstream" directions can be seen. One consists of changing the diagram type, to a histogram. This entails also changing the vertical axis, to a linear rather than a logarithmic scale. This makes the uncertainty in the last data point (given by Boehm as between 200 and 1000) much more dramatic: the last column dwarfs all the others, making the diagram woefully uninformative.

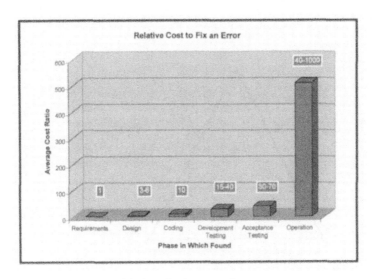

Simplified Boehm's curve - histogram

The other tendency, which eventually wins out for reasons we'll shortly explain, starts by first stripping away all of the data points, retaining only the two straight lines, which on a logarithmic scale mean two different exponents governing the exponential curve. Here is a version from 2006:

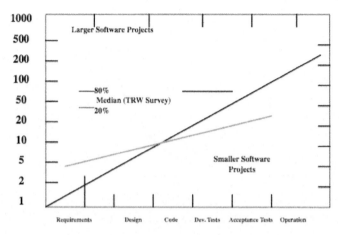

Simplified Boehm's curve - no points

But what this version gains in simplicity, it lacks in "oomph", in drama. Lines are in, but logarithmic scales are out. What would *really* have some impact is something like the following:

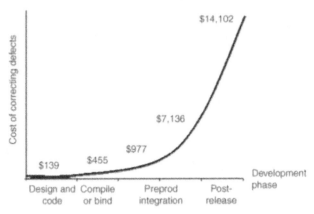

Figure 1.2 Defect correction cost profile for the software industry

Simplified Boehm's curve - no points

Never mind that important features, like proportionality on the vertical scales, or accuracy of the numbers shown with respect to the source cited (a 2001 Boehm and Basili paper, "Software Defect Reduction Top 10 List") are thrown out the window: Boehm and Basili don't quote any dollar figures in that paper. This source contains other inaccuracies, for instance claiming that "the numbers first published in 1996 were revalidated in 2001" - false on both counts.

But at least this shows the way. The curve is now looking a little *too* simple, though, with perhaps the risk that it will not look authoritative enough. Another attempt looks like this, which is a lot more impressive with its grid-and-sheets 3D aspect:

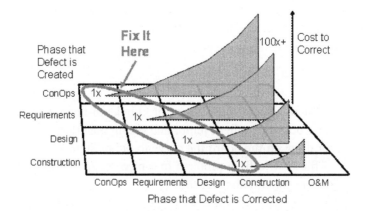

Elaborated Boehm's curve - sheets

This last variant is from a U.S. Department of Transportation technical report on Systems Engineering, credits Steve McConnell's "Code Complete" for the source, and is *nearly* accurate - it throws in a non-existent phase "ConOps" but otherwise looks fairly close to its original, which (see Appendix B for details) can only have originated in one data set, the Hughes Aircraft Study. The only little problem is that the graphs are not at all accurate representations of the Hughes Aircraft data.

Changing the topic altogether

Through all the above variants, however, one thing remains constant: the curve is still a depiction of how "defects become more expensive the later you fix them".

This seems to have changed in 2000, with the publication of Kent Beck's "Extreme Programming Explained: Embrace Change", where one chapter - title "Cost of Change" - reprised an earlier (1999) article of Beck's in "C++ Report". (The book had much more of an impact than the article.)

Here is how Beck's book tells the story:

> I can remember sitting in a big linoleum-floored classroom as a college junior and seeing the professor draw on the board the curve found in Figure 1. : "The cost to fix a problem in a piece of software rises exponentially over time..."

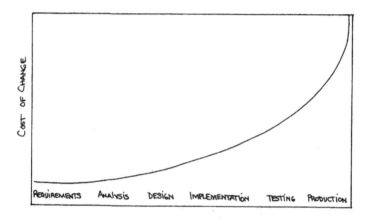

Beck's curve

It's hard to tell if the error is Beck's or his teacher's, but this change, or confusion, is quite significant.

Previously, the import of the curve had already been generalized from "this is true of defect costs on a few projects surveyed by researchers known to Boehm in 1976", to "this is true of defect costs in general". With this change, the curve's meaning changed into "this exponential increase is true of all changes to all software on all projects".

Beck didn't stop there, and claimed - based on personal experience, and not claiming any numerical evidence to back it up - that Extreme Programming "flattened the curve".

Almost single-handedly and almost overnight, Beck had framed the debate between the "traditional" lifecycle and the "upstart", rebellious strategies which would soon become widely known under the umbrella term "Agile". One of the main points of contention of the debate would be the shape of the "cost of change curve".

This, even though the curve no longer had the slightest empirical backing *as* a general observation applying to how expensive it is to make changes (of any sort, not just bug fixes) to existing software.

Reading curves

When you see a curve like the "cost of defects" curve, drawn as a continuous line, bear in mind that it's a misleading representation: the data behind the curve is actually only a few points. In this case, the horizontal axis represents the "phases" of the waterfall cycle, so that's about six points in total. The histogram representations, for all that they alter Boehm's original portrayal, are a little less misleading.

The smooth representation is a distortion, which leads you to think of the horizontal axis as "time" and invites you to view the curve as a functional: this is how the "cost of defects" graph

morphed over time into the "exponential cost of change curve"
- even though "fixing a defect" and "any kind of change to
software" are radically different kind of beasts.

The other distortion is to view such a curve, *because* it appears
smooth and equation-like, with physics-glasses on - and to think
that, like the law of gravity, it is a universal law that applies to
all software projects, everywhere, all the time.

You should cultivate a reflex of always asking this question: what
does *one* data point on this curve represent?

In the original diagram (the one from Boehm in 1976) there are
data points from several different projects plotted on the same
curve. The intention is to compare these different projects, and
the conclusion is "look, they have the same curve, more or less,
so we have uncovered a general law".

The problem, as we know, is that projects are very different from
each other: there are big projects and large projects, there are
projects with lots of defects and projects with... even greater
numbers of defects. How do we make these comparable with
each other?

Theory-laden diagrams

The only way to do that is to look, not at the *total* costs of defects,
but at the *average* cost to fix *one* defect. (You need to break
down the data even further, to show these averages based on
the "phase" when defects are detected. Few projects have data
this detailed - in fact as we saw, some projects cited by Boehm
did not.)

To get *one* data point on the Boehm curve, what you need to do is collect the *total* cost of defects detected in *one* particular phase, and divide that by the *number* of total defects.

To get valid comparisons between different projects, you also need each project to define "phase", "defect" and "cost" in the exact same way, which is not the case in Boehm's data; and that requires that you start off by knowing *what you mean* by each of these terms, which is by no means a settled issue.

But "average cost to fix one defect" is a stupid metric, as Capers Jones argues in a paper on "A Short History of the Cost Per Defect Metric" (see Jones[30]). It makes bad projects look good, and good projects look bad.

How? By failing to divide the costs of fixing into two categories: *fixed* costs of detecting and fixing defects - costs which are the same no matter how buggy or how good the product is - and *variable* costs, those which you pay for each defect.

The more defects you have, the more your fixed costs get spread around, and the *lower* your "average cost per defect". The better your quality, the fewer defects you have, the *higher* the average will be.

In Jim Highhsmith's book "Agile Software Development Ecosystems", Boehm is quoted as saying something that backs away from the "universal law" interpretation of the curve: he basically says that the better projects have a "flatter" curve, and it is only relatively unenlightened projects that had the fast-rising curve. (This is kind of an odd thing to say: in his 1976 article the steeper curves were associated with the project at the prestigious

---

[30]http://semat.org/wp-content/uploads/2012/03/a_short_history_of_the_cost_per_defect_metric.doc

IBM, and at Boehm's own employer TRW, where supposedly enlightened software engineering was the norm.)

You can see where this is leading - Jones' argument and Boehm's are squarely in conflict: *we should expect bad projects to have flatter defect cost curves*, if we agree with Jones, because each point on the curve is an average that will spread the more expensive fixed costs. And we can assume that "more enlightened" projects will have *more* investment in the fixed expenses of defect prevention activities.

Either Boehm or Jones is operating on a wrong model, and my money is on Jones being more correct (which, of course, does not mean "absolutely correct").

Boehm's assent

But let's go back to the "cost of change". What's amusing about this story is that Boehm eventually published a response to Beck, in a 2003 book co-written with Richard Turner, "Balancing Agility and Discipline: a Guide for the Perplexed". There, Boehm *fully assents* to Beck's rewriting of the curve as representative of all changes:

> The steep version of the cost-of-change curve was discovered by several organizations in the 1970s (TRW, IBM, Bell Labs Safeguard). They found rather consistently that a postdelivery software change was about 100 times as expensive as a Requirements-phase software change.

Boehm adds the following indication that a renewed inquiry may be in order:

> Considerable uncertainty has arisen over whether these escalation factors remain representative in today's software development environment.

However, this is only to dash any hope, as he immediately claims confirmation of the ancient findings:

> To explore this and related questions, [the Center for Empirically Based Software Engineering (Ce-BASE)], performed a literature search and held three e-Workshops involving people with relevant experience and data. The results tended to confirm the 100:1 ratio for large projects, with factors of 117:1 and 137:1 recorded, and a 1996 survey showed a range of 70-125:1.

This is word-for-word identical to the text appearing in Boehm's "Making Software" chapter. Sadly, these newer results are not much more credible than the older ones, as Appendix B details.

Savor the delicious irony of self-fulfilling prophecies: Beck (or his teacher) misinterpreted Boehm's curve, but by generating enough of a stir and prompting Boehm to respond as he did, was the cause of Boehm's "cost of defects" curve becoming "Boehm's cost of change curve".

This magical transmogrification is *only* possible, let us note, because the curve has 100% ideological and 0% empirical content.

The curve is only a blunt instrument of oratory: it is there, not to convey knowledge about the real world, but to win arguments.

 Key points

If a picture is worth a thousand words, a false picture is a thousand times more serious than one careless word.

Our previous encounter with the Cone of Uncertainty taught us to ask: is the graph merely conceptual, a pictorial representation of the author's opinion? Or does the author claim that there is data backing the graph?

When looking at a graph or chart, purported to be backed by empirical data, remember to ask: what specific measurement does *each* of the points I'm looking at represent?

If the picture is a curve, and it has many more data points than were actually measured, ask: was the method for interpolating the missing points actually valid?

Picture references

All pictures are used without permission, for "fair use" illustrative purposes.

The 1996 picture is from Leffingwell's "Calculating Your Return on Investment from More Effective Requirements Management".

The 2006 picture is from "The TCAT for Java/Windows User's Guide".

The 2007 "simple" picture is from McLeod and Everett's "Software Testing: Testing Across the Entire Software Development Life Cycle".

The 2007 "grid and sheets" picture is from the U.S. Federal Highway Administration's "Systems Engineering for Intelligent Transportation Systems".

Chapter 11: Rocket science and Flaubert math

The 2006 report[31] from NASA's "Independent Verification and Validation Facility" makes some interesting claims. Turning to page 6, we learn that thanks to IV&V, "NASA realized a software rework risk reduction benefit of $1.6 Billion in Fiscal Year 2006 alone". This is close to 10% of NASA's overall annual budget, roughly equal to the entire annual budget of the International Space Station!

If the numbers check out, this is an impressive feat for IV&V (the more formal big brother of "testing" or "quality assurance" departments that most software development efforts include). Do they?

Flaubert and the math of ROI

Back in 1841, to tease his sister, Gustave Flaubert invented the "age of the captain problem", which ran like this:

> A ship sails the ocean. It left Boston with a cargo of wool. It grosses 200 tons. [...] There are 12 passengers aboard, the wind is blowing East-North-East, the clock points to a

---

[31]http://www.nasa.gov/centers/ivv/pdf/174321main_Annual_Report_06_Final.pdf

quarter past three in the afternoon. It is the month of May. How old is the captain?

Flaubert was pointing out one common way people fail at math: you can only get sensible results from a calculation if the numbers you put in are related in the right ways. (Unfortunately, math education tends to be excessively heavy on the "manipulate numbers" part and to skimp on the "make sense of the question" part, a trend dissected by French mathematician Stella Baruk[32] who titled one of her books after Flaubert's little joke on his sister.)

Unfortunately, NASA's math turns out on inspection to be "age-of-the-captain" math. (This strikes me as a big embarrassment to an organization literally composed mainly of rocket scientists.)

The $1.6 billion claimed by NASA's document is derived by applying a ROI calculation: NASA spent $19 million on IV&V services in 2006, and the Report further claims that IV&V can be shown to have a 83:1 ROI (Return on Investment) ratio. Thus, $19M times 83 gives us the original $1.6 billion. (The $19M is pure personnel cost, and does not include e.g. the costs of the building where IV&V is housed.)

What is Return on Investment? Economics defines it as the gain from an investment, minus the cost of investment, divided by (again) the cost of investment. An investment is something you spend so as to obtain a gain, and a gain is something caused by the investment. This isn't rocket science but basic economics.

---

[32]http://fr.wikipedia.org/wiki/Stella_Baruk

But how does NASA arrive at this 83:1 figure?

NASA IV&V's math

NASA relies on the cost of defects "research" we've just covered.

NASA counted 490 "issues" that IV&V discovered at the requirements stage of the Space Shuttle missions, during some unspecified period between 1993 (the founding of the IV&V Facility) and 2006. (An "issue" is not the same as a defect, but for the time being we will ignore this distinction.) To this, NASA adds 304 issues found between 2004 and 2006 in other ("Science") missions. (We are also told that this analysis includes only the most "severe" issues, i.e. ones for which a work-around cannot be found and which impair a mission objective.)

We can verify that $(490+304)^*200 = 158,000$, which NASA counts as the "weighed sub-total" for Requirements; adding up the somewhat smaller totals from other phases, NASA finds a total of 186,505.

NASA also adds up the number of issues found during all phases, which is 2,239. We can again verify that $186,505 / 2,239 = 83$ and some change.

How old is the captain?

Now, the immediate objection to this procedure is that an ROI calculation involves dollars, not numbers of "issues". ROI is a ratio of money gained (or saved) over money invested, and while you can reasonably say you've "saved" some number of issues it's silly to talk about "investing" some number of issues.

We will want to "steel-man" NASA's argument. (This is the opposite of a "straw man", an easily knocked down argument that your interlocutor is not actually advancing, but that you make up to score easy points.) We will be as generous with this math as we can and see if it has even a small chance of holding up.

To rescue the claim, we need to turn issues into dollars. Let us list the assumptions that need to hold for NASA's calculations to be valid:

- there is some determinate average cost to detecting an issue
- there is some determinate average cost to fixing an issue
- if an issue is not detected at the earliest opportunity, it always ends up being detected "in the field" and its repair cost is the maximum

The first two assumptions give our steelman attempt some lee-way; not all issues need to cost the same to detect, but it has to make sense to talk about the "average cost of detecting an issue". Mathematically, this implies that the cost of fixing an issue obeys some well-behaved function such as the famous "bell curve". (However, there are some functions for which it makes no sense, mathematically, to speak of an average: for instance some "power law" curves. These are distributions often found to describe, for instance, the size of catastrophes such as avalanches or forest fires; no one would be very surprised to find that defect costs in fact follow a power law.)

The third assumption makes things even more problematic. NASA's calculations are based on hypotheticals: what if we used different assumptions, for instance that an "issue" in Requirements has a good likelihood of being found by NASA's diligent software engineers in the design phase? If all issues detected by IV&V in Requirements had been fixed in Design, then the ratio would only be about 5:1 (that is, the ratio between 200:1 and 40:1). Using a similar procedure for the other phases, we would find a "ROI" of less than 3:1. This isn't to say that my assumption is better than NASA's, but merely to observe that the final result is very sensitive to this kind of assumption.

However, we may grant that it is in NASA's culture to always assume the worst case. And anyway "up to $1.6 billion" is almost as impressive as "$1.6 billion", isn't it?

Eighy-three! For some value of eighty-three.

If we do accept all of NASA's claim, then an "issue" costs on average about $9K to detect. (As a common-sense check, note that this on the order of one person-month, assuming a yearly loaded salary in the $100K range. That seems a bit excessive; not a slur on NASA's competence, but definitely a bad knock for the notion that "averages" make sense at all in this context.)

However, note that NASA's data is absolutely silent on how much the same issues cost to fix. Detecting is IV&V's job, but fixing is the job of the software engineers working on the project.

(An "issue" is just an observation that something is wrong, whereas a "defect" is the thing software developers fix; it's entirely possible for several "issues" related to one "defect" to be corrected simultaneously by the same fix; NASA's conceptual model grossly oversimplifies the work relationship between those who "validate and verify" and those who actually write the software.)

NASA is therefore reporting on the results of the following calculation...

ROI = (Savings from IV&V - Actual cost of IV&V) / Actual cost of IV&V

where

Savings from IV&V = Hypothetical cost of fixing defects without IV&V - Actual cost of fixing defects

...and the above cannot be derived from the numbers used in the calculation - which are 1) counts of issues and 2) actual IV&V budget. Even if we do grant an 83:1 ratio between the hypothetical cost of fixing defects (had IV&V not been present to find them early) and the actual cost of fixing, we are left with an unknown variable - an unbound x in the equation - which is the average cost of fixing a defect.

This, then, is the fatal flaw in the argument, the one that cannot be steel-manned and that exposes NASA's math for what it is - Flaubert-style, "age of the captain" math, not rocket science.

Key points

When confronted with quantitative claims based on calculations, critical thinking must still apply.

Obviously, the result of a calculation can only be as good as the premises upon which the calculation is based: the GIGO principle applies.

However, it pays to also attend to the calculation itself: is it sound? Does it relate together quantities in sensible ways? (Physicists are fond of "dimensional analysis[33]" as a tool to detect bad calculations rapidly.)

Acknowledgements

Thanks to Aleksis Tulonen, a reader, for finding the NASA document in the first place, and spotting the absurdity of the ROI calculation.

---

[33]http://en.wikipedia.org/wiki/Dimensional_analysis

Chapter 12: For some value of 56

While we're on the topic of "bad math", I'd like to make a point about our apparent craving for precise statistics - and argue that it is 180 degrees from how we ought to react.

Where bugs come from

One impressively widespread quotation from a 1984 James Martin book ("An Information Systems Manifesto") gives us a precise answer to this question, with which we began this book, and at first blush leprechauns do not seem to be involved: "requirements are the source of 56 percent of all defects".

As with many of these old wives' tales, this can be used by anybody to justify any idea they support. So for instance you find instances of it in relatively recent presentations introducing the idea of "Behaviour Driven Development", strictly a 21st century idea (BDD[34]).

Let's think about this one for a minute.

We all know that body water accounts for about two-thirds of our body weight. I'm pretty sure that no one imagines that *one* human body was sampled (leaving aside how it's measured, an interesting topic in itself) to get this result.

---

[34]http://www.scribd.com/doc/54772257/Behaviour-Driven-Development

Why? Obviously because a single measurement would have left wide open the possibility that the individual in question was somehow anomalous. So, we expect that this statistic comes from taking measurements from a range of individuals, and as is often the case we expect that we'll get a normal distribution, with the most often seen value falling somewhere in the middle.

Just as obviously, there's a wide range of values that are "normal" for individuals at various ages, so we wouldn't expect that the "correct" or accepted value would be given even to within one percent; actual values range from 45% to 75%.

We would expect that any given individual's value couldn't stray *too* far from this already large range... but only because water, and in particular intracellular water, is a critical component of a human body. If we look instead at, say, body fat, individual values might range from 2% to 50%, a huge variation.

So even as a "rule of thumb" 56% is extremely over-precise, and suspect.

Sample size of one

But here's the real wake-up call: Martin's data *is* from a single "individual":

> "Figure 4.1 shows the distribution of bugs in a large bank, of the total, 56% were in the requirements document and 27% were in design."

"Defects" is nowhere near as stable a concept as "body fat" or "body water", for which you can rely on standardized definitions and off-the-shelf instruments, giving you readings in minutes: you can expect every *single* decision to attribute some defect to "requirements" or "design" or "code" could provide fodder for hours of discussion to a team of project stakeholders. (My colleague Michael Bolton calls this "the problem of counting to one" - if it's already hard to identify *one* defect, counting *many* of them is going to be a fraught enterprise.)

The software engineering profession *as a whole* needs to feel ashamed that it will so readily repeat, as if it were a universal truth, something that is only a half-baked figure from a single project in a single business, and what's worse on the strength of a book published when the discipline was less than half its current age, and with a title that promised emotional appeals would dominate over factual findings.

But maybe I'm being too harsh - we all know we use only 10% of our brains, right?

Poor requirements

And as long as we're talking statistics, an illustration of the "base rate neglect fallacy" - and one more reason why you shouldn't mindlessly repeat other people's numerical claims.

A widely circulated one is that "71% of failed software projects suffer from poor requirements". Imagine for just a moment that it's well-supported, and in fact true. Would you then be able to infer any *causation* from this figure, such as the equally widespread "71% of project failures are *caused* by poor requirements"?

That would be the case only if the percentage of *all* projects that suffer from "poor requirements" is much different from 71%!

If around two-thirds of all software projects have some character-istic X, and this characteristic has no effect on project outcomes, then when you sample failed projects only you are going to get the same two-thirds ratio. This number could be anything else and the previous sentence would still hold. (In fact, completely different numbers are also seen in the literature: the Chaos Report is claimed as saying 20-25% - one of these claims must be wrong.)

In other words, even if true, this statistic offers no support at all to the hypothesis that "poor requirements" (whatever that is supposed to mean) is a good *predictive* test of software project outcomes.

A software triumph

It is more than a little ironic that this very book is made possible by an information infrastructure so powerful that it truly deserves to be called a "software triumph", even as present-day articles continue to bemoan a "software crisis".

So, for instance, not only am I able to scour the whole Web for instances of the "71% of project that fails do so from poor requirements" meme, I can even use the date stratification trick to pinpoint the exact source.

This is a CIO Magazine article from 2005 by a Christopher Lindquist, and the only source cited is "Analysts report that..."

As you can verify by searching[35] for one variant or another, the claim is nowhere to be found before this date, but becomes widespread afterwards; the claim is *immediately* picked up by various secondary sources, many of which quote it verbatim, but with even more changing the wording slightly.

The fun thing is that the attributions change more recently, in 2011:

- one Victor Font[36] attributes it to "Grady, 1999"
- the NASCIO conference[37] 2011 page attributes it to "Butler Group"

These apocrypha are interesting to study, because they reveal something of the telephone game's routing circuits. For instance, the Butler Group misattribution is likely due to a blog[38] which cites both CIO magazine *and* Butler Group, for two distinct (though equally suspect) claims. (This is kind of bad news for the US, in this foreigner's opinion - NASCIO is supposed to be "representing the CIOs of the States".)

In the Victor Font case, you can trace some of the spread, such as to a company called StratNet[39], apparently not related to Mr Font, simply by noting that Font is misspelling the name of "Liffingwell", instead of "Leffingwell" - I assume this is the Dean Leffingwell I've already encountered previously.

---

[35] http://bit.ly/wXtoB7
[36] http://www.linkedin.com/groups/Whos-Blame-Troubled-Projects-IT-51825.S.39024193
[37] http://www.nascio.org/events/2011Annual/agenda.cfm
[38] http://basftw.blogspot.com/2010/06/something-for-weekend-new-in-at-1.html
[39] http://www.stratnet.ca/?c=blog&l=en&art=20110305-1

This is all fun and games, though, until you get the idea of running your search not in Google, which indexes the "layman's Web", but in Google Scholar: the more hallowed residence of Science.

There you will find at least one academic paper[40] (I didn't have the heart to look for more) picking up the 71% meme. Look at the attribution: "...echoing earlier work by Lindquist (2005)..." Yes, this is how the careless, unsourced and unverifiable assertion of an editorialist becomes the "work" of an academic peer: by the adoubement of scholarly parentheses.

Here is at least one case of cross-species contagion, raising the specter of Homo Academicus' vulnerability to what we might have hoped was a disease confined to Homo Consultantus.

"Contagion" seems like an appropriate word, and I'm pretty sure that models from epidemiology would be useful in studying this kind of thing in quantitative terms: it feels a lot like the spread of a disease.

With Michele Lanza's "Requiem for Software Engineering[41]" in mind: software engineering died of a contagious disease, and the epitaph on its grave shall be "Requirements are the source of 56% of all bugs in any project, for *some* value of 56."

---

[40]http://proceedings.informingscience.org/InSITE2008/IISITv5p543-551Davey466.pdf

[41]http://soft.vub.ac.be/benevol2011/abstracts/Lanza.html

Key points

Any statistic about software projects that is more precise than "around some multiple of 5%" is likely to be a Leprechaun.

The wonderful thing about over-precise statistics is that they are the easiest to expose as being Leprechauns, as you can trace their spread from one dubious source to another.

However, as with virulent diseases, it is important to stop them before they reach the world of academic research and thereby gain such legitimacy that they can no longer be eradicated.

Chapter 13: The cost of bad research

Previously, we saw how the "defect-cost-increase curve", whose empirical basis appeared to fade into anecdote as soon as we looked at it a little closely, morphed over the latter decades of software engineering's history into the fully generalized (but still no better supported) "cost of change curve".

I want to take a closer look at the implications of this telephone game: what it says about the state of research in the software engineering discipline.

Uncritical thinking

We have previously encountered the "Citation Needed" heuristic, which states that "if you *can't* cite a source for your claim, then your claim is *probably* bogus".

But it scares me that some people apparently operate under the *reverse* heuristic: "if you can cite a source for your claim, the claim is probably true". Lest you think I'm making this up, one blogger has even made up an acronym for it: INBSIYCNTS[42], "It's Not BS If You Can Name The Source".

This is madness.

---

[42]http://blogs.popart.com/2009/02/inbsiycnts-1/

The blog post in question is about the "cost of defects" claims, and according to the blogger "This fundamental concept is attributed to Robert Grady", who studied it while working at Hewlett-Packard. Deploying the usual arsenal of the Leprechaun hunter leads to an article, "Dissecting Software Failures", by the same Grady; of the study done at HP, Grady writes:

> "The data for this example is taken from a detailed study of defect causes done at HP. In the study, defect data was gathered after testing began. [...] **This study didn't accurately record the engineering times to fix the defects**, so we will use average times **summarized from several other studies** to weight the defect origins.

I want you to read this several times until it sinks in, especially the bits in bold. The emphasis is mine. "We didn't bother to study claim X because we knew it was already proven", is what this article cited to support claim X basically says.

Once a claim has taken root, it starts to inform later study: this is what brings Thomas Kuhn in *The Structure of Scientific Revolutions* to argue that there is no such thing as "pure" observation, and that all measurement is "theory-laden".

Extraordinarily suspect claims

One reaction to "Leprechauns" that I'm anticipating is this.

"Okay," people will say, "you have shown that some of the older studies weren't really up to par. But still, it's obvious and well supported by everyday experience that defects are harder to fix the longer they stick around, and you are not showing any really good studies that suggest otherwise. And have you seen *this* newer reference, which does have confirming data?"

The problem is that this game of shifting goalposts can go on forever. The title of the book isn't (just) whimsy. I've chosen it quite deliberately because one of my crucial arguments is going to be about burden of proof, and I know what to expect there because I've followed what happened to people who tried to debunk ESP and UFO claims: the silly claims *will just keep on coming.*

So, I'll agree that the burden of proof is on me, for the first few studies, to show that there are some shenanigans going on. Empirical data will be assumed innocent until proven guilty - to start with.

But after a few instances of something turning out to be a leprechaun, it is no longer necessary to respond in detail and specifically to every single challenge of the type "Have you seen the data in *this* paper, which reports on a detailed count of leprechauns in County Wicklow?"

We should stop responding not because the papers' methods or inferences are faulty, but *because there are no freaking leprechauns!*

People are prone to confirmation bias, and we have seen in lavish detail how such a claim as the rising cost of defects will take root, and in effect become a self-fulfilling prophecy. So, after enough "studies" (or really, references to studies, since it's rarely the studies themselves that are bad but what later authors want to make them claim) are discredited, it's time to shift the burden of proof.

We can now dismiss any new *citations* along the lines of "studies say" that don't add a great deal more about why the studies in question are credible. We've shown that many authors cite carelessly, citing papers they haven't read for instance, or citing people who are not themselves credible sources but who are in turn citing other research. So we now insist that the bar is higher: fool me once, shame on you, fool me twice, shame on me.

This doesn't mean that we should dismiss new *studies* out of hand, as a matter of principle, but we should insist that they specifically address the reasons which made the older studies unsatisfactory.

The claims have become suspect enough to fall under a maxim similar to that used by critics of purported UFO sightings and other wild claims: "extraordinary claims require extraordinary evidence", something that we could express as "once-suspect claims require particularly careful evidence".

Terms of inquiry

But surely, you may object, the situation in software engineering is different: there are no leprechauns, to be sure, but *there are* such things as defects and fixing defects? Surely a dollar is a dollar, and it's clear that fixing defects has a cost?

Yes and no. But mostly no!

The first thing you have to do, whenever you start thinking about this kind of thing, is furrow your brows and take a hard look at each of the *words* in that phrase you're thinking about: "cost", "fix", "defect". (Okay, the furrowing is optional.)

Think about "defect", and think about all of the ways that two people might reasonably disagree about what counts as a "defect" and what doesn't. For instance, if you are a developer, have you ever argued with a user or a manager about whether something was a "bug" or really an "enhancement" or even in fact a "feature"?

Here is what my friend Michael Bolton (to whom I'm indebted for some of the ideas below, and an expert on testing), had to say about "defects" within literally seconds of thinking about the term: "When is it a defect? When the programmer notices his own typo and fixes it before the build? When he fixes it after the build? When someone else notices it? What happens if they notice it during a pair programming session? Is it a defect then? If you happen to link to a bad library, is that a defect? A link to a bad library might not manifest a bug for a while; then it might manifest dozens of different problems when someone tries to call a particular function. Is that dozens of defects, or just one?"

Definitional debates of this kind are commonplace. (And, generally, developers hate them with a vengeance for being huge time wasters.) But if you want to count defects, you first have to decide what (literally) counts as one. We have a hard time even agreeing among a single team on what counts as a defect - in fact I'm pretty sure my own thinking has changed over the years, so I'm not even agreeing with myself.

Before you could validly generalize results from empirical observation of "defects", you would have to be sure that two researchers looking at "defects" meant the same class of events in the world, in much the same way that scientists looking at "atoms" or "birds" should look at the same class of thing in the world.

And notice the distinction above: *events* are even slipperier things to deal with than *things*. Defects are not "things" - they are, in a nutshell, human decisions, which places their study squarely in the realm of sociology; a discipline in which no "computer scientists" or "software engineers" generally receive training.

And that's just the start of our difficulties, since the same analysis can be performed for the next word, "fixing". (Left as an exercise for the reader.)

Even "cost" is not as transparent as it looks: an easy way to recognize that is to look at any study, and observe that this is almost never measured as-is, but in fact replaced by "time spent" as a more measurable proxy. "Cost" is actually a fairly sophisticated notion of accounting, another discipline in which few software professionals are ever trained.

Even measuring how people spend their time is a tricky business: you have to decide on a particular way to do that, which include sitting behind people's backs with a stopwatch, or having people fill out time sheets or forms.

Each of these ways may have associated difficulties, not the least of which is interfering with what it's measuring: people can get nervous when someone is timing them with a stopwatch, for instance, or complain that they spend so much time filling out time sheets that the time sheets need a new category for that. (I'm speaking from personal experience.)

The upshot of all the above is that unless you are very careful to ensure a clear connection between the terms in which you phrase your claims, the precise "objects" designated by these terms, and the inferences that you ultimately derive from observations of these objects, any "research" you spend time on is only going to result in confirming your existing prejudices.

Research standards

The prevalence of bias is one of the main reasons why research papers submitted to peer reviewed journals usually have to follow a certain form, and (in some disciplines, such as medicine) this form is ruthlessly enforced: your abstract must state the conclusions and some key features of your statistical analysis, you must describe your sample and your procedures, and you must carefully note any "threats to validity".

"Threats to validity" is a shorthand for the following question: "is our experiment a 'smoking gun' for whatever it is we were trying to reveal, in other words does it rule out most of the alternative hypotheses that we could think of?" (This subdivides into further, more technical categories, such as "external validity" and the ever thorny "construct validity", on which I urge you to read Cem Kaner's paper: "Software Engineering Metrics: What Do They Measure and How Do We Know", see Metrics[43].)

Often, the hard work in research isn't in performing the experiment and collecting data (that tends to be grunt work, in fact, in most disciplines). The hard work consists of designing the

---

[43]http://testingeducation.org/a/metrics2004.pdf

experiment that will rule out the most alternative explanations for what you see happening (or think you see happening).

If your paper doesn't conform, it will be rejected. That is, if the review process is doing its job correctly - but that's more a feature of the socio-political side of research, and we won't go into that here.

But we have now reached the most pressing problem in software engineering: low standards for research publications. Most of what passes for "research" in the discipline is *ridiculously careless* with respect to examining the "terms of inquiry".

Key points

Lack of critical thinking has allowed wrong claims to take root in the discipline and become entrenched.

In light of this situation, we can no longer be content with incremental additions to research that continues past tradition. Studies can no longer claim to measure "defects", for instance, without a full-on investigation of whether what the term means has been pinned down enough to allow measurement. (The same goes for e.g. "productivity".)

Chapter 14: Raising the bar

Two modest proposals for publications on software development

- Any paper containing a first-degree reference to "the software crisis" should be rejected summarily.
- Any author citing another paper should be required to provide proof that they a) possess a copy of that paper, b) have read that paper, c) have read the paper carefully.

The most economical means of proof is to include a short quotation from a paper which is available online for free.

For "paywalled" papers, or those only available in print or on microfiche, stronger proof would be required, such as an MD5 hash of part of the article text, different from all such hashes provided by other authors.

Will you take the pledge?

The above two suggestions, though not quite up to Swiftian[44] standards, are nevertheless impractical: they would cause publication in software engineering to more or less grind to a halt.

---

[44]http://en.wikipedia.org/wiki/A_Modest_Proposal

Perhaps a slightly less outrageous idea would be to offer a pledge, and only suggest that a few brave authors proclaim their intent to adhere to it, hoping that by their example the movement might snowball:

> As an author writing about software engineering, I am committed to providing the best grounding for any factual claims I make or support. To that end I will:

- only cite papers that I have in fact personally read
- refrain from indirect quotation (or other 'telephone game' variants)
- make it clear whenever I'm citing opinion or indirect quotation, as opposed to original research
- cite page and section numbers when available, and always when citing books
- whenever possible, cite papers freely available online in full text versions
- refrain from citing obscure or non peer-reviewed sources
- check that the data I'm citing actually supports the claim
- look for contradictory evidence as well as supporting, to avoid confirmation bias
- only make prudent claims, and present all plausible threats to validity.

Chapter 15: A new model of inquiry

> Our industry will start to mature when it stops thinking about programming as being like something else, and when it realises that the only thing that programming is like is programming.
>
> – Nat Pryce

Here is my big, bold thesis. The current approach to inquiry embodied in the discipline of software engineering is a dead end. We can't begin to make progress until and unless we understand what's so seductive about the current research paradigm and thoroughly destroy that appeal. This has been in large part the mission of this book.

Too many still think that "software engineering" should something like medicine, studying the impact of various "substances" (test-driven development, code inspections) on our pathologies (poor quality, budget overruns, and so on), using the golden standard of Randomized Controlled Trials.

Software development will not usefully be studied with such an approach. It needs to be studied with tools that borrow as much from the social and cognitive sciences as they do from the mathematical theories of computation.

We need to stop thinking of "code as a naturally occurring substance" and focus more on the social and conventional aspects of software. We need to stop using terms like "requirements" and "architecture" and "testing" and "performance metrics" as if they *defined* the reality of software development, and take a closer look at programmers and their interlocutors and how they really work. Better and more useful terms will emerge from that inquiry.

The Ouroboros effect: circular causation

Software engineering is a social process, not a naturally occurring one - it therefore has the property that what we believe about software engineering has causal impacts on what is real about software engineering.

One reason why fixing defects late can cost more is that the process makes it more expensive to fix defects later, as one participant in an online discussion observed: "if a defect is found later in the our process, at least 2 QA analysts are involved: one to find the defect and another to confirm...".

Why does the process make it more costly to fix defects later? Because the process is built on the assumption that it makes sense to invest heavily in business analysts at the early stages (to get the requirements right), not so much into development (they're an expensive commodity) and heavily in testing (we all know these developers still write lots of bugs, they can't be trusted); so in that process "a project manager schedules out time and assigns the defect out to a developer, possibly not the one that introduced the defect gets the assignment to fix it".

The causation is circular: of course if you measured the time to fix bugs under that process you would find the cost rising according to the phase when bugs are detected, because the process is built on this very assumption.

From Requirements To Negotiation

I have worked more than once on software development efforts where one of the input to my or my team's work was a document which included pixel-painted (think Photoshop) screen mockups.

Implicitly, this created an expectation that any deviation in placement, color, text etc. in the software as implemented constituted a "bug". In at least one of these projects I behaved, without prompting, as if that expectation constrained my work. Later, I tended to question that assumption, but still I met folks from "the non-technical side" who also subscribed to that assumption, to the extent of asking the team for corrections. In some cases, I or the team invested quite a bit of effort into replicating the exact look of these mockups, even though they conflicted with standard user interface guidelines of the target platform.

In retrospect, this strikes me as egregiously stupid. People unqualified to do so were designing user interface elements poorly, and people more qualified than them to correct these deficiencies were prevented from doing so.

Some might be tempted to shrug this off and reply with the punchline of a standard doctor joke: "Don't do that then."

Or you could see that as one of the inevitable problems arising from the notion of "requirements".

Creating mockups to communicate is not intrinsically a bad idea. But, as we are subject to confirmation bias, there's always a risk that we will stop at our first design attempt and become reluctant to ask if there are better ways to achieve the same goals. Making these first ideas very detailed; putting them into a document; and especially blessing that document with the label "requirements" are all moves which make further revision less likely, and put us more at risk from confirmation bias.

The first two moves may be survivable, they are just tactical aids to thinking about the design decisions involved - but because the term "requirements" comes bundled with a whole set of assumptions about the "social contract" of software development, this last move is much more difficult to undo.

Putting something in a "requirements" document is generally taken by the various parties involved to mean "the developers may no longer question this".

At this point the conversation has changed domains. Before, it was about "what's the best way to achieve purpose X or Y". After uttering (or writing) the word "requirements", it has become (at least in part) about "who's allowed to tell whom what to do". I suspect that when too much of this has taken place, projects are basically doomed.

This is one reason I've been curious for some time now what would result from systematically expunging the term "requirements" from our vocabulary and using "negotiation" instead. Wouldn't that be a great experiment?

The cliffhanger

Unfortunately, I must bring this book to a close without answering the question raised at the start of this chapter, the one implied by the whole enterprise: if Software Engineering has reached a dead end, what is to replace it, and what is a better way of investigating the reality of software development?

I have some ideas about what the fundamental attributes of such a model are (what even I, after all this work, almost called the "requirements" for the model):

- it must acknowledge the human nature of the task, and draw on the cognitive sciences and facts about human brains and minds
- it must also be rooted in the closest thing we have to "natural laws", the mathematical properties of computation (Turing's demonstration of the halting problem, and so on)
- it will have to be in part experimental, studying minute details "in the laboratory", and in part naturalistic, drawing on observations of "real world" software development

We cannot leave this enterprise to academia: that system's inertia is too great. I believe that many of us will have to become scientists, and *study* software development even as we practice it. (In fact, my experience with Agile and Lean thinking and discourse has convinced me that we *all* need to become better scientists; software development efforts present us with such unique and complex challenges, generating large amounts of data (and noise), that we all need to become better at generating and validating, on the fly, hypotheses about "what's going on here".)

My hope is that a few (perhaps many) years down the road, someone - perhaps even myself - will find an urgent need to write another book, chronicling the beginning of that exciting revolution.

Appendix A: bibliographical analysis of the 10x files

This appendix is a more detailed explanation of how I went about the bibliographical work summarized in the "10x files" chapter.

My research started with Curtis 1981, chronologically the first of the sources claimed as support for 10x. My concern was one of verification. Specifically, I supposed that for each of the sources listed I could make an assessment of the empirical data contained therein, and note threats to validity listed by the author.

By following the list of references forward in time, I could note which later sources referenced the earlier ones, and which of these sources reported on observational setups designed to address such threats to validity. **This is the standard process of "incremental" science.**

I was most interested in the following particulars of each data set:

- sample size
- task type
- population type (students or professionals)
- measurement performed (e.g. time to complete task, LOC per period)

- effect being studied
- magnitude of variation reported

Sample size mattered because a large sample should in general carry more evidential weight than a small sample (leaving aside considerations such as selection biases). Also, as discussed below, the "best-to-worst ratio" measurement may be sensitive to sampling effects, and in particular it is likely that a larger sample will exhibit a greater range than a smaller sample.

Task type mattered because certain tasks may a) be more intrinsically subject to variability than others - debugging is well-known as this type of very open-ended activity, irrespective of the programmer's skill, and b) not necessarily take up a substantial portion of a typical programmer's time. More generally, if we observe substantial variation in performance when looking at a narrow part of the diverse activity we call "programming", there is **no guarantee that this observation will generalize to the whole of the activity**.

Population type is a common issue encountered in this type of research. Students are commonly used as study subjects because researchers typically have ready access to students at affordable cost ("convenience samples"). However this can lead to distortions of the results, if there are systematic differences between students and professionals which can bias observations; for instance for our purpose, if the performance of students can be expected to be more variable than that of professional programmers.

It is important to know what is being measured and how, since these are typically major factors considered in the "threats to validity". Also, the empirical data will have different weight depending on whether (as in Sackman et al. 1968) the variation is observed while studying some other effect, or whether the variability is the direct object of the study.

Finally, of course, the quantitative result must be compared to the "order of magnitude" claimed in 10x.

Questions of indirection

Early in my investigation it became apparent that some of the references above **did not directly allow these assessments; most commonly because they were not primary but secondary sources**, that is, publications where the authors asserted the 10x claim by reference to an earlier source.

Therefore I added to my concerns the following:

- is the reference a primary or secondary source?
- if secondary, what were the authors' original conclusions, irrespective of the source's?
- is the citation to a data set already cited elsewhere in the list?

This last concern was important because **I wanted my degree of belief to be determined by the quantity and quality of the empirical evidence**, rather than by the number of apparently authoritative assertions of the claim; I wanted therefore to guard against "double counting" of some data sets.

Summary results

Below are my findings, summarized for the references above, other than Sackman 1968.

Supporting sources for 10x, table 1

Reference	Direct?	Task type	Sample size
Curtis 1981	Y/N	Debugging	27
Mills 1983	Y	unknown	unknown
DeMarco and Lister 1985	Y	program to spec	166
Curtis et al. 1986	N	n/a	n/a
Card 1987	N	project	unknown
Boehm and Papaccio 1988	N	n/a	n/a
Valett and McGarry 1989	N	project	150
Boehm 2000	Y	project	161 *(projects)*

Supporting sources for 10x, table 2

Reference	Population	Measure	Effect studied	Variation
Curtis 1981	pros	time-to-complete	LOC on debug time	22:1 and 8:1
Mills 1983	unknown	unknown	unknown	10:1
DeMarco and Lister 1985	pros	time-to-complete	workplace	5.6:1
Curtis et al. 1986	n/a	n/a	n/a	various
Card 1987	pros	LOC per staff hour	none	not claimed*
Boehm and Pa-paccio 1988	n/a	n/a	n/a	various
Valett and Mc-Garry 1989	pros	LOC per staff hour	none	not claimed*
Boehm 2000	pros	manager's evaluation	none	not claimed

* - see discussion below; a textual claim of "6 or 10 to 1" is found in the primary

The quest for primary sources

One direct observation emerges from the summary: most of the sources in the list of above references were secondary, and provided no direct information on the empirical data or the methodology for its collection. So I undertook to find and obtain the primary sources, that is, the publications where the data was described for the first time, along with the research methods.

Here is a quick summary of the results of this chasing down exercise:

From Curtis 1981: the origin of the data is Sheppard et al. 1979. (Bill Curtis is a coauthor of the original research; one of the "et al.")

From Curtis et al. 1986, section II.A:

- the first source is Sackman et al. 1968 (already in our list)
- the second source is Curtis 1981 (already in our list)
- the third source is Boehm 1981
- the fourth source is McGarry 1982

From Card 1987: it is unclear what the primary source is. However, "Figure 3" which appears to support a claim of large productivity variation (although no specific ratio is claimed in the text) reports identical averages to Valett and McGarry 1989; I therefore considered plausible that either the latter was the primary source, or that both shared an identical primary source.

From Valett and McGarry 1989: close examination of the text (figure 2.1) answers the above question, citing the primary source for the "Profile studies" which originate the graphs for individual variation. This primary is again McGarry 1982.

From Boehm and Papaccio 1988: this cites two primary sources. In section 1.2: "the (Brown-Lipow, 1973) comparative experiment showed a 10:1 difference in error rates between personnel.". The other reference is in section 2.1.1, which cites Sackman et al. 1968 (already in list) and refers to a 26:1 variation in productivity.

It's a judgement call whether to consider Curtis 1981 a "primary" source. It reports on data which were, by design, not included in the discussion of experimental results in the 1979: they are data from a "pretest", a preliminary task used by the Sheppard et al. to anticipate problems that might arise in the context of the experimental task. (This was indeed the case: Curtis 1981 reports that the program initially selected was "too difficult", leading the experimenters to switch to a different program.)

The curious reader should also be aware than an earlier and substantially different version of Card 1987 *under an identical title* is available on the Web; this 1985 version is not paywalled, but the 1987 version is. Some remarks in an earlier essay of mine were addressed to Card 1985 which I had mistaken for Card 1987. Such is the kind of problem you run into in this kind of bibliographical work.

A better list: primary sources with empirical evidence

Summarizing the above, here is the list of all the primary sources I was able to identify with discernible empirical data:

- Boehm, Brown and Lipow, 1973
- Sheppard et al. 1979
- Curtis 1981
- McGarry 1982
- DeMarco and Lister 1985

Mills 1983 does not directly mention or indirectly reference empirical data. Two references, Boehm 1981 and Boehm 2000, *do* constitute a treatment of empirical data, but this data is **not relevant to the 10x claim for individuals.**

Only one of these sources (DeMarco and Lister 1985) is from the original list of 8 sources claimed to confirm Sackman et al 1968.

References (original)

(McConnell 2010) "What Does 10x Mean? Measuring Variations in Programmer Productivity", in "Making Software", O'Reilly, 2010, p567

(McConnell 2011) http://forums.construx.com/blogs/stevemcc/archive/2011/01/09/of-10x-how-valid-is-the-underlying-research.aspx (retrieved 27/01/11)

(Mall) Fundamentals of Software Engineering, Rajib Mall, Prentice-Hall of India, 2004

(Huang) http://www2.cs.uh.edu/~jhuang/JCH/SE/estimation.ppt (retrieved 27/01/2011)

(Dickey) Dickey, Thomas E. 1981. "Programmer Variability," Proceedings of the IEEE, 69, 7, (July): 844-845.

(Sheppard et al. 1979) S. B. Sheppard, B. Curtis, P. Milliman, and T. Love, "Modern coding practices and programmer performance," Comput., vol. 12, no. 12, pp. 41-49, 1979

(Boehm 1981) B. W. Boehm, Software Engineering Economics. Englewood Cliffs, NJ: Prentice-Hall, 1981.

(McGarry 1982) F. E. McGarry, "What have we learned in the last six years?" in Proc. 7th Annu. Software Engineering Workshop (SEL-82-007) (Greenbelt, MD: NASA Coddard Space Flight Center), 1982.

(Brown and Lipow 1973) Brown, J. R., and M. Lipow, The quantitative Measurement of Software Safety and Reliability, revised from TRW Report No. SDP-1776, August 1973, TRW Software

(Boehm, Brown and Lipow, 1976) Barry Boehm, J. R. Brown, M. Lipow, "Quantitative Evaluation of Software Quality," Proceedings of the 2nd International Conference on Software Engineering, San Francisco, California, 1976, pp. 592-605

(Weinberg and Schulman 1974) Weinberg, Gerald M., and Edward L. Schulman. 1974. "Goals and Performance in Computer Programming." Human Factors 16, no. 1 (February): 70-77.

(PROMISE 1981) http://promisedata.org/repository/data/coc81/coc81_-1_1.arff (retrieved 29/01/11)

(PROMISE 2000) http://promisedata.org/repository/data/nasa93/nasa93.arff (retrieved 29/01/11)

(Kaner 2004) http://www.kaner.com/pdfs/metrics2004.pdf (retrieved 29/01/11)

(Sackman and Grant 1967) Grant, E. E., and H. Sackman, "An Exploratory Investigation of Programmer Performance Under On-line and Off-line Conditions", IEEE Transactions on Human Factors in Electronics, Vol. HFE-8. No. 1, March 1967, pp. 33–48.

(Lampson 1967) Lampson, B. "A critique of 'An Exploratory

Investigation of Programmer Performance Under On-line and Off-line Conditions'", IEEE Transactions on Human Factors in Electronics, Vol. HFE-8. No. 1, March 1967, pp. 48-51.

References (from McConnell 2010)

(Augustine 1979) Augustine, N. R. 1979. "Augustine's Laws and Major System Development Programs." Defense Systems Management Review: 50-76.

(Boehm and Papaccio 1988) Boehm, Barry W., and Philip N. Papaccio. 1988. "Understanding and Controlling Software Costs." IEEE Transactions on Software Engineering SE-14, no. 10 (October): 1462-77.

(Boehm 2000) Boehm, Barry, et al, 2000. Software Cost Estimation with Cocomo II, Boston, Mass.: Addison Wesley, 2000.

(Card 1987) Card, David N. 1987. "A Software Technology Evaluation Program." Information and Software Technology 29, no. 6 (July/August): 291-300.

(Curtis 1981) Curtis, Bill. 1981. "Substantiating Programmer Variability." Proceedings of the IEEE 69, no. 7: 846.

(Curtis et al. 1986) Curtis, Bill, et al. 1986. "Software Psychology: The Need for an Interdisciplinary Program." Proceedings of the IEEE 74, no. 8: 1092-1106.

(DeMarco and Lister 1985) DeMarco, Tom, and Timothy Lister. 1985. "Programmer Performance and the Effects of the Workplace." Proceedings of the 8th International Conference on Software Engineering. Washington, D.C.: IEEE Computer Society Press, 268-72.

(Mills 1983) Mills, Harlan D. 1983. Software Productivity. Boston, Mass.: Little, Brown.

(Sackman et al. 1968) Sackman, H., W.J. Erikson, and E. E. Grant. 1968. "Exploratory Experimental Studies Comparing On-line and Offline Programming Performance." Communications of the ACM 11, no. 1 (January): 3-11.

(Valett and McGarry 1989) Valett, J., and F. E. McGarry. 1989. "A Summary of Software Measurement Experiences in the Software Engineering Laboratory." Journal of Systems and Software 9, no. 2 (February): 137-48.

Appendix B: bibliographical analysis for the "defect-cost-increase curve"

The older set of references examined is from Boehm's 1981 book "Software engineering economics", p.39; the curve itself is on the next page; and for Boehm 1976 from Boehm's chapter in the book "Making software".

The more recent set is from Boehm's chapter in the book "Making software", and from slide decks published on the Web site of Construx, a consultancy that has compiled extensive bibliographies on topics related to estimation, software quality and more.

The older references

Boehm 1980

This is given as "Developing Small-Scale Application Software Products: Some Experiment Results" from IFIP Proceedings.

In fact that is definitely the same study, and possibly the same text (the abstracts are almost word for word identical) as "An

Appendix B: bibliographical analysis for the

Experiment in Small-Scale Application Software Engineering",
IEEE TSE 1981.

The main difference seems to be that the latter is available online
(for a fee via IEEE's CSDL), but not the former...

Boehm claims the earlier paper as reference for a 5:1 ratio
between cost to fix defects in "Requirements" phase compared to
"Acceptance testing" phase. (The later paper in fact claims only
a 4:1 ratio. This may not seem like a big deal, but any reduction
in the effect size, given the small sample studied, means it is
that much more likely that the variation arose by pure chance
or because of some influence other than "phase the defect was
detected".)

Boehm only gives 2 data points when reproducing the diagram
in his books, or in the much more recent book "Making Software", p.163. One for the "requirements" phase and one for the
"acceptance test" phase.

The subjects are two teams of first-year graduate students, in
the Fall. One team using Pascal and the other Fortran. This
is problematic for generalization: these would be very young
people working on their very first programming project.

The workload during the project was self-reported, collected by
having students fill in weekly time forms; the average time spent
on the project ranged from 5 hours per student in week one to
15 hours per student in week 11.

It's difficult to tell what yields the two data points with a 4:1
ratio. There is no discussion of how many defects were handled
in each phase, only of the total aggregate cost of "fixing" efforts.
(Remember that the cost-to-fix curve is supposedly about the

average cost to fix *one* defect.)

Boehm notes a "deadline effect" resulting from the introduction of two review activities at weeks 3 and 6 of the 11-week project, and attributes the limited ratio of costs to the deadline effect. In fact "fixing" effort is (as one might expect) much higher for both teams in the weeks that follow the review activities.

The single week in which the most effort was spent was - as you might guess - the final week. This is less an empirical finding about how costs are distributed throughout a software projet, and more an empirical finding about how students allocate working time.

If you look at Fig 2. of the paper, which I reproduce below, you can see that cost-to-fix ratios are not rising linearly as the usual curve suggests.

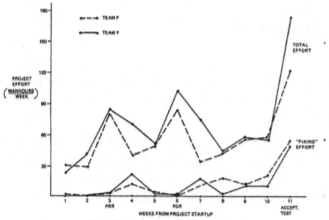

Fig. 2. Distribution of project effort by week.

"Distribution of effort" chart

The curve is sawtooth-like. Week 4, early in Design phase, has about 20 manhours of fixing, compared to about 50 manhours in week 11. (That's only a 2.5:1 ratio between Design and Acceptance Testing, which is much less than it "should" be.) But Week 10 "fixing" effort for instance is quite a bit less than Week 4 "fixing" effort.

And in fact you have to wonder why Boehm included only 2 data points in the book diagram: the effort data was collected for each of the 11 weeks.

The problem, of course, is that if Boehm had reproduced all of the data points, his book diagram would have shown a sawtooth curve, not the smoothly rising linear curve he in fact shows (linear on the log scale, so smoothly *exponential* on a normal scale).

Verdict: leprechaun sighting.

Stephenson 1976

Titled "An analysis of the resources used in the safeguard system software development", this paper was published in the proceedings of ICSE (available online from ACM: free to members, for a fee otherwise).

Boehm obtains three data points from this study on Bell Lab's Safeguard project, a "cost to fix" of about 3 midway through Requirements, and of about 50 to 100 during the span from "Development" to "Acceptance testing".

Searching the paper for what figures are used to yield these data points is a fruitless and frustrating exercise. The paper uses the term "defect" very little, and elsewhere the more informal "problem" is used but in none of these cases in reference to the cost of corrective activities.

The paper itself specifically disclaims any attempt at breaking down costs to the level that would support Boehm's claims:

> The data presented addresses total system software development as opposed to individual programmer or even group productivity levels. [...] The inter-dependence of actual coding and testing upon the many other activities, such as system requirements generation and design [...] make it difficult and of questionable value to isolate to a unit or program level.

Verdict: leprechaun sighting.

Boehm 1976

This is simply titled "Software engineering", appeared in IEEE Transactions on Computers, and is available online for free at the IEEE, in a stunning departure from their usual policy.

Boehm claims this as the source for "a summary of current experience" at TRW. Data points are supplied for each phase, and there are error bars for all the points (except one, and we'll come back to that exception).

As the title suggests, this isn't a paper covering one focused empirical study. It's a broad overview, attempting to provide a definition of the term and a survey of the field at that time, and of what prospects lay ahead for it.

The cost-of-defects curve is on page three, just after a page showing "hardware-software cost trends" (a chart which we know cannot be strictly empirically derived, since it purports to extrapolate said trends to the mid-1980s, ten years after the paper), and the usual representation of the Software Development Life Cycle, also known as "waterfall".

No numerical data is supplied at all concerning TRW. Nor is any further reference given suggesting where the TRW data might be found.

Verdict: leprechaun sighting.

The TRW study

Even though we can quickly dismiss the previous paper, a few things here need to be noted. First, TRW was where Boehm *worked*, so that's where it was easiest for him to get at studies showing what he wanted to show; even, if necessary, ahead of publication.

Second, the study he needed did in fact exist: it is the rather massive TRW "Software Reliability Study", also available online for free TRW[45]. If Boehm had cited that, we would have the "needle in a haystack" problem, in spades, as the study runs to 350 pages, which I've only briefly skimmed.

Page 44 of the study has an interesting tidbit: "coding errors have been shown by Shooman and Bolsky to be less costly to diagnose and correct than design errors", the opposite of the rising-cost-of-defects claim. The TRW study doesn't disagree with this conclusion, apparently.

---

[45]http://1.usa.gov/yX7srV

Looking at Section 4, you find that the study looked at many of the questions, on a defect-by-defect basis, that would confirm the claims in the diagram: when the error was detected, when it was introduced, how long it took to fix.

The study provides a diagram of this last data on page 144: it charts "mean problem closure time" as a function of "problem priority". The authors don't seem to be very interested in closure time, which only rates a brief analysis (compared e.g. to the dozens of pages, with sophisticated regression charts, of the relation between defects and code complexity). The chart has data for four test phases (validation, acceptance, integration, "operational demonstration"). It does not jump out from the diagram that times-to-fix are longer in later than in earlier phases.

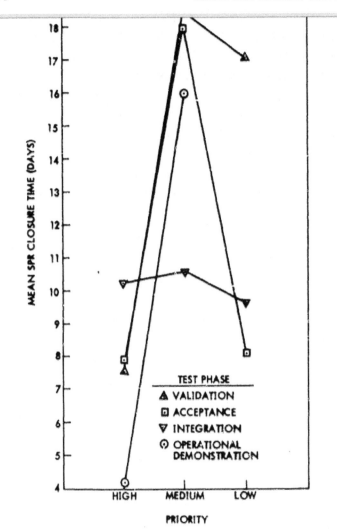

"Mean SPR closure time" chart

Page 38 adds this: "...errors attributed to a source in software requirements were probably recorded as design errors in this investigation, although no problem report specifically cited requirements in either project's data." The TRW study did *not* look at the cost to fix defects originating in the requirements phase.

Verdict: leprechaun sighting.

And... One more thing.

Remember these error bars we noted earlier in Boehm 1976? There's only one data point that doesn't have them. It's "coding", which is associated with a "relative cost to fix" of exactly 1. In other words, this diagram is claiming to know *exactly* how much it costs to fix a defect detected during the coding phase. Whereas the costs to fix defects detected earlier or later are not known with much precision.

Later versions of this diagram, in particular that appearing in Boehm's 1981 book, do not have this feature: they fix defects spotted at *requirements* as having a baseline cost of 1, and show a cost of 10 (exactly: no error bars) for errors spotted during coding.

We can imagine why the TRW data point associated with "requirements" would need an error bar: it is perforce speculative, since the TRW study didn't record that cost data. So Boehm is saying "I guesstimate that correcting an error in the requirements phase would be about one-tenth the cost of correcting it while coding".

But it's embarrassing to have this kind of strongly pointed out by the Coding=1 association. I suspect that's why later versions fix Requirements=1. Which doesn't matter, of course, since the diagrams chart *relative* cost to fix.

Still, I can't help but see this tiny change as significant.

Daly 1977

This is E.B. Daly's "Management of Software Development", a 1977 paper in IEEE Transactions on Software Engineering, available online for a fee.

Boehm claims this as the source for two data points, one about 30 to fix a defect in the unit testing phase, the other in the range 150-300 to fix a defect after deployment.

The paper discusses some statistics from project experience at GTE. It is largely prescriptive rather than descriptive; it presents a "methodology" for the software development cycle. The empirical results are interspersed with the description of this recommended approach, with extremely sparse descriptions of the data collection methods.

There is relatively little discussion of the cost of fixing defects; and one illustration, Fig. 13, which I'm reproducing here. (They say that "a picture is worth a thousand words". Fig. 13 consists of fifteen words, and adds no discernible value over and above a sentence of text containing the same fifteen words. It's tempting to call Fig. 13 a waste of 985 words, close to 99% of its potential value.)

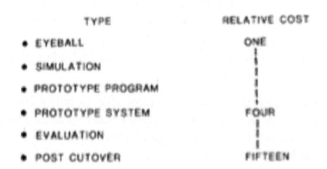

Fig. 13. Cost of finding a software bug.

"Cost of finding a software bug" chart

The text says: "The development cost required to detect an error by reading code is approximately equal to 25 percent of that required to detect the same error via machine debugging. This statistic was gathered from two projects", one large and one small.

One should keep in mind, when reading this, that in the 1970s computers had much more limited capacities, and therefore the expense referred to above is mostly that of the computer time required for debugging runs. In fact, here is the sentence immediately preceding the one I quoted above: "Code reading and mental testing should always be employed prior to object-machine testing in order to minimize usage of expensive machine time." So this 4:1 differential would either not exist anymore nowadays, or arise from very different causes.

Toward the end of the paper there is somewhat more extensive discussion of the cost of fixes, and another reference to Fig. 13 says: "The development cost required to detect and resolve a software bug after it has been placed into service is thirty times larger than the cost required to detect and resolve a bug during the early 'code reading' phase."

As you can see from the rather simplistic Fig. 13, only a ratio of 15:1 is claimed, and the comparison isn't really concerned with life-cycle phases, but with the type of activity which results in detecting bugs.

No detailed data is provided, nor any information about the manner of collecting this "statistic". It's hard to treat it as much more than (possibly informed) opinion.

Verdict: leprechaun sighting.

Fagan 1976

Titled "Design and code inspections to reduce errors in program development", this is available online for free: rejoice!

Boehm claims this as the source for five data points labeled "IBM": at the Requirements, Design, Development (i.e. Unit) testing and Acceptance testing phases, plus a relatively wide spread (100 to 1000) post-deployment.

Four of these data points only appear in the 1981 and later versions of Boemh's diagram, even though the study cited is the same: the 1976 version only shows the last of these data "points", in fact a very spread-out range (100 to 1000).

The paper opens with a paean to discipline, and I can't resist quoting this bit: "An ingredient that gives maximum play to the planning, measurement, and control elements is consistent and vigorous *discipline.*" Ah, sweet, vigorous discipline! The emphasis is Fagan's, by the way.

But let's move on to the cost of rework. On page 185, the claim is presented as a bald assertion: "The cost of reworking errors in programs becomes higher the later they are reworked in the process, so every attempt should be made to find and fix errors as early in the process as possible."

(I'm pointing this out to show that this isn't really an "investigation" in the usual sense; Fagan starts out already well convinced of this claim, and his research isn't intended to find out or to explore, or even to replicate - as far as this topic goes.)

For once the manner of collecting data is described in some detail. The data provided comes from a sample, "a piece of the design of a large operating system component". The process presented by Fagan includes three inspection steps: one after "design complete", one code inspection, and one unit test inspection, "done to see that the unit test plan had been fully executed".

Note that there is no requirements inspection, and it is not clear where Boehm is getting the first data point, the one corresponding to the earliest phase; or the last data point, the 100-to-1000 spread.

And here is the section on the cost of rework: "The error rework in programmer hours per K.NCSS found in this study due to I1 was 78, and 36 for I2 (24 hours for design errors and 12 for code errors)."

In other words, Fagan finds a 2:1 ratio *in the other direction* from that claimed in the rising-cost-of-defects curve! (Though this isn't really cost-to-fix per defect, but cost-to-fix relative to the overall code size, but it's suggestive that what Fagan measured isn't quite what Boehm claimed.)

The rest of the paper - which is mostly prescriptive, rather than an empirical study - does not discuss further empirical data on the cost of rework.

On page 202 there is one sentence which one could be vaguely tempted to interpret as support for the final 100-1000 data point: "This [inspection process] results in much lower cost than in the 'old' approach, where the cost of error rework was 10 to 100 times higher and was accomplished in large part during the last half of the schedule."

Of course this would be a criminally loose interpretation: what is being compared is overall cost, not cost per defect; what is being compared is an older method with a newer method, not two distinct phases. We'd better assume that Boehm was not getting that data point from that sentence.

Verdict: leprechaun sighting.

The newer references

Lindner and Tudahl 1994

This is "Software Development at a Baldrige Winner", appearing in Proceedings of ELECTRO'94, describing practices at IBM's Rochester installation. This is available online for a fee to members of the IEEE, but infuriatingly is *not* available through the IEEE Computer Society's Digital Library.

As to its credibility: it's a PowerPoint!

There isn't one page of narrative text. Therefore, obviously, no information on what the authors mean by "defects" or "cost of defects", no information on sample sizes, populations, etc.

The only reference to the defect-cost-increase claim is a diagram, with unlabeled axes and the title "cost of defects". This diagram says "inspection: X, test, 13X, field 92X". (This is mistakenly reported as 117X in the eWorkshop paper, other sources report it as "9X then 13X" - also mistakenly.)

Yes, unlabeled axes: remember in high school when you'd get a slap on the fingers for failing to label your axes? Well, what is cited as "research" in our field isn't up to high school standards.

Verdict: leprechaun sighting

McGibbon 1996

This is given as "Software reliability data summary", a Data & Analysis Center for Software (DACS) Technical Report, supposedly presented during a 2002 "eWorkshop" (an online instant-messaging discussion among experts).

Boehm's 2010 chapter claims that this reference shows "a range of 70-125:1", however this is inconsistent with two versions of the "minutes" from this eWorkshop, both of which report a "100:1 factor", see eWorkshop[46].

The DACS' own Web site does not list any Technical Report by that title, see DACS[47]. The author, Thomas McGibbon, is the

---

[46]http://www.cs.umd.edu/~mvz/pub/eworkshop02.pdf

[47]http://www.thedacs.com/techs/tr.php?orderby=date

Director of DACS, a US DoD contractor "chartered to collect, analyze, and disseminate information relating to the software domain".

Only one Technical Report is listed with a date of 1996 and author McGibbon, and this is "A Business Case for Software Process Improvement", available in a 2007 revision on the DACS Web site, see BizCase[48].

This 2007 reference contains one 100:1 claim which is consistent with the eWorkshop minutes, and with a date (1995) which does not rule out its being already present in the 1996 version. However, it cites no other evidence in favor of the defect-cost-increase claim, *and* this one claim is presented as an "estimate", not the result of any measurement.

Verdict: leprechaun sighting.

Leffingwell 1997

This is given as "Calculating the Return on Investment from More Effective Requirements Management," American Programmer, volume 10, issue 4.

The article has been reprinted online in IBM DeveloperWorks, see Calculating[49].

The first section title is "The Software Crisis Continues Unabated", which is a preview of things to come: the article is an editoral piece, not a research report.

In typical telephone game fashion, the only relevant evidence provided is an older citation:

---

[48]http://www.thedacs.com/techs/abstract/347616

[49]http://www.ibm.com/developerworks/rational/library/347.html

> Studies performed at GTE, TRW, and IBM measured and assigned costs to errors occurring at various phases of the project life-cycle. These statistics were confirmed in later studies.

The "later studies" are in fact the same as the earlier studies, since the reference provided is to a well-known 1988 Boehm paper "Understanding and Controlling Software Costs" that has the dubious honor of being frequently used as a reference for both the 10x claim *and* the defect-cost-increase claim.

But this 1988 article in turn provides no evidence of its own, only referring back to the same studies cited in Boehm's 1981 book.

Verdict: leprechaun sighting.

Grady 1999

This is "An Economic Release Decision Model: Insights into Software Project Management" from Proceedings of the Applications of Software Measurement Conference, 1999 - an SQE conference.

This paper is available nowhere online. It was presented at one of the first editions of a little-known SQE conference on "Applications of Software Measurement".

This paper is often cited as one of the recent sources for the "rising cost of defects" claim; people even quote specific "cost multipliers" depending on phase that come from a chart in this paper. Unfortunately, its extremely limited availability makes it hard to check what data it may refer to.

After a lot of digging around, one finds that the author was with Hewlett Packard, and that the study in question is probably the same one that was referred to in one chapter of his book on "Practical Software Metrics", titled "Dissecting Software Failures". If this is indeed the case, then our search for verifiable information is over, as one online article, Dissecting[50] gives details on the study, including the following quote on page 2:

> "The data for this example is taken from a detailed study of defect causes done at HP. In the study, defect data was gathered after testing began. [...] **This study didn't accurately record the engineering times to fix the defects**, so we will use average times summarized from several other studies to weight the defect origins."

(Read this several times until it sinks in, especially the bit in bold.)

Verdict: leprechaun sighting.

Humphrey et al 1991, Willis et al 1998

Though these two references are seven years apart, they refer to the same long-running process improvement initiative: "Software process improvement at Hughes Aircraft", in IEEE Software, Volume 8, issue 4, tells the beginning of the story; the rest is in "Hughes Aircraft's Widespread Deployment of a Continuously Improving Software Process", Software Engineering Institute, paper 115.

---

[50]http://findarticles.com/p/articles/mi_m0HPJ/is_n2_v40/ai_7180006/

Both are available online, see HughesOne[51] and HughesTwo[52].

The first reference is focused strictly on Hughes' ascension from CMMI level 2 to level 3. It provides no numerical data on the cost per defect as a function of phase.

The second reference is *much* more interesting. It is the only one, out of all the literature surveyed for evidence of the defect-cost-increase, which in facts attempts to fill the entire "matrix", crossing "phase when defect was introduced" with "phase when defect was corrected". The defects database analyzed included close to 70,000 defects at the time the study was written up.

This is the only data set that looks like a credible source for the "grid and sheets" design variant of the Boehm curve; no other has this matrix structure.

The problem is that the ratios are far, far from what Boehm claims, and far, far from what the "grid-and-sheets" variants depict!

Look at the bigger chart, representing defects introduced in "Requirements Analysis". Numerically, fixing the cost of a defect at 1 in "Requirements Analysis", it only costs 6 times more to fix it in the "Functional Test" phase, in the pre-1991 data set. In the post-1991 data set, the worst ratio is 11:1, between "System Test" and "Requirements".

Worse for the "defect-cost-increase curve", the data do not bear out a monotonically increasing cost phase after phase: it is again a sawtooth curve!

---

[51]http://www.ipd.uka.de/mitarbeiter/padberg/lehre/sqs07/
HumphreySnyderWillisSOFTWARE1991.pdf
[52]http://repository.cmu.edu/sei/115/

There is also a lot of variance in the data, not at all like the smooth exponentials suggested by the various pictorial representations of the curve. If you look at the smaller charts, there are indeed some large inter-phase ratios in other columns, but there are also some much smaller ones.

METRIC –
Average Cost to Fix Defects Found in Each Phase

Effort to Correct Requirements Defect (staff-days)

Phase Detected and Corrected	Before 1991	1991 and Later
Req Analysis	0.36	0.05
Preliminary Design	0.95	0.15
Detailed Design	0.46	0.07
Code	1.58	0.17
Unit Test	0.75	0.25
Integration Test	1.07	0.51
Functional Test	2.00	0.47
System Test	0.81	0.58
Maintenance	0.65	no data

Weighted average = 0.84
(Total 810.42 staff days of rework divided by 964 defects. Excludes defects detected in phase.)

Figure 25   Analysis of Quality Indicator data resulted in requirements review efficiency improvements that reduced overall effort.

Average Cost to Fix Defects Found in Each Phase

Verdict: a leprechaun sighting, but at least this is clearly "a guy in a leprechaun suit", not "a blurry picture which could be anything including a leprechaun".

Online references

Appendix C - Conceptions and invention of waterfall

Invention of waterfall

Prior to 1987 only a single article citing Royce is from someone other than TRW personnel. One paper cites Royce from an internal TRW publication, with the same date as the Westcon venue generally cited. This a joint effort with Loesh from JPL, and JPL is the one exception to the TRW rule. It's probably fair to say that up to 1987 Royce is purely TRW lore.

No less than 10 papers mention "Boehm's Waterfall": Lehman 1984, Overstreet et al. 1987, Harbison-Briggs 1990, Chroust et al. 1990, Conger et al. 1991, Chroust 1994, Moretton 1997, Burback 1998, Kuiper 2001, Portougal 2006.

(Blum 1993 has "Boehm's waterfall" but it is to distinguish it from "Royce's waterfall")

Conceptions of waterfall (articles between 1970 and 1989)

There is no indication that authors from TRW have direly misunderstood Royce: the occasional references to Royce's "5 principles" establish that TRW personnel have a good grasp on what his article actually said.

However none of the citing papers from that twenty-year period uses anything other than the "cascade" picture which is Royce's Figure 3 (or sometimes Figure 2).

The Liu article from 1989 suggests that Royce wasn't opposed to a conception of his model as one where "the completion of one phase leads to another" and as a "manufacturing model" - this article was "recommended by Royce", a footnote says.

Williams (TRW) 1975

- does not refer to waterfall by name
- pic on p3 is the 8-step cascade
- "the rather conventional step-wise production process illustrated"
- "admittedly a gross simplification"
- "contains the essential ingredients"
- then cites all 5 of the sections of Royce (do it twice, etc.)
- "not necessary to elaborate further upon these important principles except to state that they [...] have come to be integral to our development approach"
- "much progress is possible through concentrated attention on the front end of the production process" (in conclusions)

Bell and Thayer (TRW) 1976

- no pic
- top down approach over bottom-up
- "design-to" requirements doc, "code to" design doc

- succession of documents leads designers through top-down process
- explained by Royce without military jargon
- few projects map nicely onto that scheme

Tausworthe (JPL) 1976

- 5-step cascade pic on p18, not citing Royce
- the Royce reference is for a later, indirect Royce quote: "Until coding begins, documentation is the specification and is the design. If documentation is bad, the design is bad."
- refers to "several mutually interacting activities"
- "the fundamental, guiding principle [...] is the top-down procedure"
- diagram on p337 makes clear the sequence is "per phase", where "phase" means "a portion of the program" - thus, somewhat incremental
- schedule diagram on p349 shows substantial overlap in activities ("phased concurrency") overall

Boehm (TRW) 1976 ("Software Engineering")

- pic of 7-step cascade with iterations between steps, not sourced
- does not mention waterfall by name
- does not cite Royce 1970 (but a different Royce paper on "problems stemming from a lack of a good requirements")

Boehm (TRW) 1983

- pic of 7-step cascade with iterations between steps
- pic of 7-step cascade with "excessive iterations" (Fig 3 of Royce)
- paper is " one of a series of efforts at TRW to define such a set of principles, beginning with a set of five principles formulated by Royce in 1970 and refined into different sets of principles [...] in subsequent efforts"
- the "waterfall" chart is Figure 2, Royce is not cited
- "the major products of each phase must be thoroughly understood, and preferably documented, before going to the next one"
- however "emphasis above on phased development does not imply that a project should defer all coding until every last detail has been worked out"
- "several refinements of the waterfall approach [...] require code to be developed early" - prototyping, incremental development, scaffolding

Boehm (TRW) 1984 ("Prototyping")

- no waterfall pic
- Royce cited alongside two other papers (Benington 56, Hosier 61)
- three approaches, Build and Fix, Specify, Prototype
- waterfall is Specifying, and evolved "to avoid the problems encountered in Building and Fixing"

- "encounters difficulties in application areas in which it is hard to specify requirements in advance [...] most frequently in human-machine interface systems"

Loesh (JPL), Reifer, Jacobs (TRW) 1984

- no pic
- no mention of waterfall by name
- the form of the citation is particularly interesting:

Royce, W. W. "Managing the Development of Large Software Systems: Concepts and Techniques." TRW Software Series Publication No. TRW-JS-70-01, August 1970.

Penedo (TRW) 1985

- "the TRW software development methodology, which covers the entire project life-cycle [...] originated in Royce 1970 and has undergone constant evolution"
- pic in Figure 2 of a 10-step cascade heavily modified from Royce's Figure 2
- no mention of waterfall by name

Overstreet 1987

- pic is 7-step cascade reproducing Boehm 1976
- legend: "Boehm's waterfall model"
- "the original treatment [...] is given in Royce 1970"

- "Boehm expands each step to include a V&V activity to cover hi-risk elements, reuse considerations and prototyping"

Boehm 1987 ("Software process management")

- introduces the three papers in a ICSE session
- Benington, Hosier, Royce (cf. his 1984 paper)
- "Royce's 1970 paper is generally considered to be the paper which defined the stagewise waterfall"
- "Royce's paper already incorporates prototyping as an essential step compatible with the waterfall model."
- "The primary additional contribution of Royce's Figure 3 is in the explicit treatment of iteration and feedback"
- "One frequent objection to the waterfall model is that it forbids prototyping. People interpret it to say, "Thou shalt not write one line of code until every detailed design specification is complete." Royce's Figure 7 shows that this was not the intent."
- "Although these three papers may be of considerable interest for historic perspective on our understanding of the software process, I do not think that is their primary value. Their main value is their continuing relevance today. Most of the specific guidance they provide on requirements analysis, prototyping, early planning, precise interface specifications, lean staffing in early phases, core and time budgeting, objective progress monitoring, integration planning and budgeting, support software preparation, documentation, test planning and control, and involving the customers and users, can be used as well today as at

the time they were written. They stand today as the record of thoughtful people summarizing the lessons they had learned,in the hopes that those of us who came along later would be able to repeat the positive software engineering experiences from history rather than the negative ones. I hope you will be able to benefit from them."

Boehm 1988 ("Spiral")

- explicit contrast with waterfall
- "original treatment" in Royce 1970
- provided two primary enhancements to stagewise model:
- feedback loops betwen (preferably adjacent) stages
- "build it twice" prototyping step
- largely consistent with top-down as discussed by Mills
- some attempts ran into difficulties, resulting in "risk management variant" supposedly discussed in Boehm's 1975 "Software Design and Structuring" and Boehm 1976 (it's hard to find the relevance of these two citations)

Davis 1988 ("A comparison of techniques...")

- pic on p2 is 5-step cascade with feedback loops
- cites Royce 1987/70
- waterfall model "characterize[s] the series of software engineering phases"
- dings waterfall for lack of symmetry, showing a V-model to fix that

- "the requirements phase is of extreme importance", must yield "a complete description of what the software will do without describing how it will do it"

Davis et al. 1988 ("A strategy for comparing...")

- pic is 7-step cascade with feedback loops
- "defined as early as 1970 by Royce and later refined by Boehm in 1976"
- most standard e.g. military methodologies follow some variation of waterfall

Humphrey 1989

- no pic
- "outside the research community, much software process thinking is still based on the waterfall framework, as described by Win Royce in 1970"
- cites Royce 1970/87 (as two references)
- "does not adequately address the pervasiveness of changes in software development"
- "unrealistically implies a relatively uniform and orderly sequence of development activities"
- "does not easily accommodate such recent developments as rapid prototyping or advanced languages"
- "provides insufficient detail to support process optimization"

- "Over-reliance on the waterfall model has had several unfortunate consequences. First, by describing the process as the sequence of requirements, design, implementation, and test, each step is viewed as completed before the next one starts. The reality is that requirements live throughout development and must be constantly updated. Design, code, and test undergo a similar evolution. The problem is that when managers believe this unreal process, they require that design, for example, be completed before implementation starts. Everybody who has ever developed much software knows that there are many tradeoffs between design and implementation. When the design is not impacted by implementation, it means that either the design went too far or the process was too rigid to recognize and adjust for implementation problems."

Liu 1989 ("A formal model")

- no pic: "it has been reprinted so often we will not reproduce it here"
- cites 1987 reprint for pic source
- ms is **recommended by Royce** to IEEE, so R presumably approves of:
- "views software development as a manufacturing process"
- "each step is a phase, and the completion of one phase leads to another"
- "each phase has inputs from a previous phase and outputs (some of which are deliverables), that it produces"
- "model is often shown with back pointing arrows as well as forward pointing arrows, acknowledging that the

manufacturing model captured in the waterfall chart is not precise, and that previous phases may be returned to"

Weitzel 1989

- no pic
- waterfall not mentioned by name
- "System development life cycles (SDLCs) originated when most systems were Transaction Processing Systems. Methodologies like Pride, Spectrum, and SDM appeared in the early 1970s. These methodologies and other SDLCs are usually variants of Royce's or Boehm's life cycles."
- "Many organizations execute SDLC phases sequentially, with a sign-off after each phase, an approach that is suitable for many TPSs."
- "Unfortunately, knowing information requirements in advance is unlikely; straight- forward design is rare, even with TPSs; and sign-offs invite difficulties. Therefore, Royce and Boehm allow for iteration. In practice, however, people resist admitting mistakes; iterating is politically and economically difficult; and people still assume specifications must precede system building."

Vickers-Benzel 1989 ("Developing Trusted Systems Using DOD-STD-2167A")

- pic is 5-step cascade with loops
- cites Royce 1970
- "the major difficulty with the waterfall model is that it does not include backtracking to correct problems"

- "systems developed using the waterfall model suffer from what has come to be known as "snap shot" specifications [...] the implemented operational system often has little resemblance to the designed and specified system"
- "the model works well in projects where the problem is familiar in all phases"
- used as a reference to present the Spiral model as preferred

Kameny et al. 1989 ("Guide for the management of expert systems development")

- pic is 8-step cascade with loops sourced to Boehm 1988 "A Spiral Model..."
- extensive description of how phases feed into each other
- "does not work well for some classes of software, particularly interactive end-user applications for which the user interfaces and decision support functions may be poorly understood"